Wolverhampton

The way it was...

A scene of activity and tranquillity all at the same time in the middle of Wolverhampton! It is about 1959 as the trolleybuses, including a recently rebodied example from Charles Roe, glide to and fro along the busy Lichfield Street, while relaxing on the park benches in the Horsman Gardens (now called St Peters Gardens) are Wulfrunians watching 'The Big Squirter' performing. This fountain is a memorial to a wealthy local dignitary, and is inscribed 'This fountain erected by public subscription in grateful recognition of the generosity of the late Philip Horsman JP who presented the adjoining Art Gallery and other philanthropic gifts to the town of Wolverhampton.' *D. R. Harvey collection*

Wolverhampton

A nostalgic tour by tram, trolleybus and bus

Part 2
The northern routes

David Harvey
and
John Hughes

·ROAD TRANSPORT HERITAGE·
from
The NOSTALGIA Collection

First published in 2002

British Library Cataloguing in Publication Data

A catalogue record for this book is available from the British Library.

ISBN 1 85794 192 6

Silver Link Publishing Ltd
The Trundle
Ringstead Road
Great Addington
Kettering
Northants NN14 4BW

Tel/Fax: 01536 330588
email: sales@nostalgiacollection.com
Website: www.nostalgiacollection.com

Printed and bound in Great Britain

A Silver Link book
from
The NOSTALGIA *Collection*

Abbreviations

AEC	Associated Equipment Company
BCN	Birmingham Canal Navigations
BET	British Electric Traction
BMMO	Birmingham & Midland Motor Omnibus Company
DS&WT	Dudley, Sedgley & Wolverhampton Tramways
ER&TCW	Electric Railway & Tramway Carriage Works
FEDD	Front Entrance Double Decker
GWR	Great Western Railway
LMS	London Midland & Scottish Railway
LNWR	London & North Western Railway
MCCW	Metropolitan-Cammell Carriage & Wagon Company
MoWT	Ministry of War Transport
PSV	Public Service Vehicle

SOS	Shire's Own Specification
UEC	United Electric Car Company
WDET	Wolverhampton District Electric Tramways
WMPTE	West Midlands Passenger Transport Executive

Seating capacity codes

H30/26R	Highbridge, upper saloon capacity 30, lower saloon capacity 26, rear entrance
H-/-RO	As above, but open staircase
H-/-F	As above, but front entrance
B38R	Single-decker bus, capacity 38, rear entrance
B-F	As above, but front entrance
B-C	As above but centre entrance

Contents

All that was Wolverhampton: Sunbeam W4 trolleybus 442 (EJW 442) stands at the Merry Hill terminus not long after receiving its second body and re-entering service on 1 August 1960. *D. R. Harvey collection*

Preface

This is the second of three books dealing with the municipal public road transport operations of Wolverhampton Corporation. The area covered in this volume is roughly the third of the town in a sector from the west, with the Jeffcock Road, Merry Hill and Finchfield trolleybus services, around to the bus routes using the Cannock Road corridor. Missing from this book are the Whitmore Reans trolleybus services, as well as the bus services that used this Victorian suburb as a stepping stone to Codsall and beyond; these will be tied in with the cross-town Darlaston trolleybus routes, which will appear in Part 3.

Each chapter deals with one sector of Wolverhampton and shows the wide variety of modes of road public transport used through the 20th century, from the early reliance on electric power through to the diesel-engined buses of today. Each of the road 'corridors', and the routes that used them, varied enormously in its character, just as the trams, trolleybuses and buses were products of their time. The original tram and replacement trolleybus services covered in this second volume range from the intensely urban, with tightly packed Victorian terraces, through to the more prosperous areas such as Tettenhall Road, with their wonderfully preserved Regency terraces. Yet at the other extreme the rural delights of southern Staffordshire, into which the green-and-straw-painted buses worked in some cases for more than 50 years, stand as a constant reminder of the enormously wide-ranging environments that were worked by Wolverhampton Corporation.

As a result, the photographic coverage of the outer suburbs and surrounding countryside, where it exists, is frequently sparse, and pictures have been selected to show the vehicles at their best in the nostalgic street scenes that encapsulate the historical and social context of the time. This does not mean that where appropriate a photograph of just a bus is not included, but generally the vehicle, be it tram, trolleybus or bus, is shown in its street scene and placed in its geographic and historic situation. Suitable 'past and present' comparisons have been made throughout the book, revealing that while in some cases the changes in the urban landscape have been dramatic, in others nothing has altered; what is strange is that redevelopment can affect just one side of a road, leaving a strange juxtaposition between the old and new.

Wherever possible the photographs have been chosen because they have not been used before, although in certain cases, because of their historical importance, pictures that have been previously published have been given a second airing. There are gaps, particularly in the suburban and rural bus services, for as in Part 1 there are pictureless 'voids' that remain unfilled. The photographs show the way in which transport has materially affected the areas through which it passes as well as illustrating the developments and changes in Wolverhampton itself.

Acknowledgements

Both authors have an extensive collection of Wolverhampton Corporation photographs that have been acquired over the years, and these serve as the basis for this second Wolverhampton volume. The collections of Alan Broughall, Clarence Carter, Alan Cross, Simon Dewey, Jan Endean of Eardley & Lewis photographic studios, Robin Hannay, Roy Marshall, Les Mason, Douglas Nicholson, Robin Oliver, Paul Roberts, Mike Rooum, Ray Simpson, Bob Smith, Roger Taft, the late Ray Wilson, and Deryk Vernon have all been a source of most useful photographs, as have all those unknown photographers who supplied the late Bob Mack with negatives. Older photographs have come from commercial postcards and from those wonderfully evocative plate photographs taken by Bennett Clarke of the life and times of everyday pre-war Wolverhampton. We obviously apologise sincerely if we have missed anyone from this long list. The late Cliff Brown's superb trolleybus photographs, all taken between 1958 and 1967, capture a time of transport as well as more obvious social change, between 'You've never had it so good' and 'the Swinging Sixties'. We would like to thank Richard Weaver and Diana Harvey for their proof-reading, and both Pam Hughes and Diana Harvey for putting up with countless meetings, for their tea and sandwich making, and for their tolerance in allowing us to trawl through boxes of photographs scattered over tables, chairs and carpets.

A definitive bibliography is virtually impossible, but the PSV Circle publication *PD6* on West Midlands municipalities, and *2PD13* on the West Midlands PTE, have provided valuable vehicle information, while the highly recommended *A History of Wolverhampton Transport* Volumes 1 and 2 by Paul Addenbrooke, published by the BTHG, are well-researched factual accounts of the development of the Corporation's services. In addition, there is a wide variety of local history books that are too many to mention, but which contribute to the understanding of the changes in Wolverhampton, as do the Alan Godfrey reprinted Ordnance Survey maps, the originals dating from the Edwardian era.

Finally, thanks are due to Paul and Tina Archer of 'The Model', Langley, near Oldbury, for their tolerance and splendid libations.

David Harvey, Dudley
John Hughes, Wolverhampton

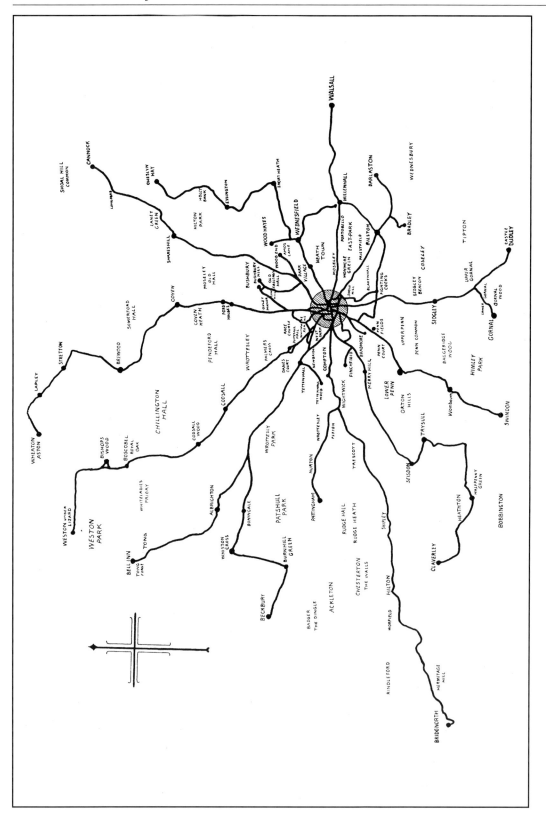

Routes operated by Wolverhampton Corporation Transport Department. The routes in the northern half of the town included in the book are those serving Merry Hill in the west to the bus services on Cannock Road in the east.

Introduction

Later trolleybus developments

Despite the increase in motorbus routes, petrol-engined buses and bus operating mileages, it was the growth in the Corporation's trolleybus system that really gripped the imagination. After the final conversion of tram services to trolleybuses mentioned earlier, there was a huge development of trolleybus routes between 1932 and 1935, when the last main trolleybus route was introduced on the system. New services were opened on the western side of the town to Penn (10 October 1932), Bradmore via Jeffcock Road (10 April 1933), Merry Hill and Finchfield (8 November 1933), Oxbarn Avenue (11 February 1934), Penn via Penn Road (8 April 1935), and Jeffcock Road via Great Brickkiln Street (8 November 1937).

Throughout this period the Corporation's standard trolleybus was the six-wheeled double-decker, continuing the link with Guy Motors and its faithful BTX model. Between 1926, when the famous trolleybus 33 was delivered, and the delivery of the 83-91 batch of Dodson-bodied trolleys at the start of 1933, the BTX model had a monopoly in Wolverhampton. Amazingly, 78 (UK 9978), a Guy-bodied Guy BTX of 1931, was discovered at Callan near Kilkenny, and in June 1990 was returned to the Black Country Living Museum in Dudley. It is not known why a Wolverhampton trolleybus finished up in the Irish Republic, and particularly this vehicle, which was extremely elusive during the latter part of its service career and was never apparently photographed in service.

A new local PSV product came from the Sunbeam Motor Company, which, in an attempt to diversify away from its ailing, large quality car production and stave off the threat of bankruptcy, turned to making trolleybuses. The company's standard six-wheel trolleybus was the MS2, of which Wolverhampton received the prototype in 1931, but surprisingly only another eight of this successful model. Wolverhampton meanwhile purchased nine of the 12 low-chassis-framed MS3s that were constructed during that model's curtailed production run, the MS3 being abandoned when Sunbeam eventually brought in the receivers in 1934. In addition, the Corporation bought all seven of the Sunbeam MF1 single-deckers built between 1932 and 1935.

There was a 'sea change' in policy after the end of 1936, when the first of the four-wheeled Park Royal-bodied Guy BTs (234-238) and Sunbeam MF2s (239-244) were delivered, and such was their success that no more six-wheelers were ever ordered. From then on the undertaking standardised on the Guy and Sunbeam four-wheelers, with either Beadle, Park Royal or Charles Roe 54-seater bodies. The last two batches of five trolleybuses were ordered to full peace-time specification, and were almost all received between February and April 1942. However, 290 (DDA 990), the last of the Park Royal trolleybuses, did not arrive until October 1942, which was almost exactly a year after the prototype Ministry of War Transport (MoWT) 'utility' body had been built on an 'unfrozen' Leyland 'Titan' TD7 to become London Transport's STD 101 (FXT 405). Numerically, the last of Wolverhampton's 'pre-war' trolleybus fleet, Roe-bodied 295 (DDA 995), chassis number 13120, was also the last pre-war four-wheel trolleybus chassis to be built by Sunbeam Commercial Vehicles.

Standardisation in the bus fleet

The contemporary bus fleet, however, showed a distinct change of allegiance from the archaic-looking six-wheeled Guy CXs of the late 1920s, after an uncertain period during the Depression years when a variety of locally produced Sunbeams, AJSs and Guys were purchased. In 1934 a pair of single-deck Daimler COG5s with fluid flywheels and Wilson pre-selector gearboxes were bought, and these were so successful that they eclipsed the newly

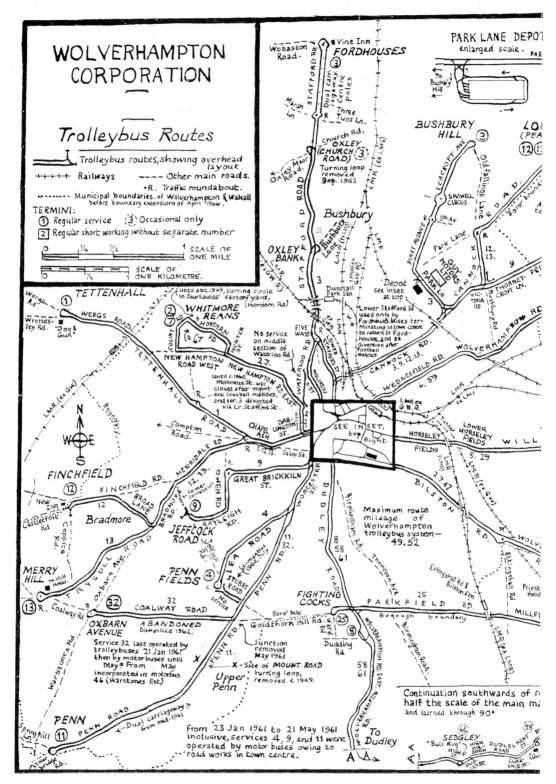

Wolverhampton Corporation trolleybus routes. *E. K. Stretch*

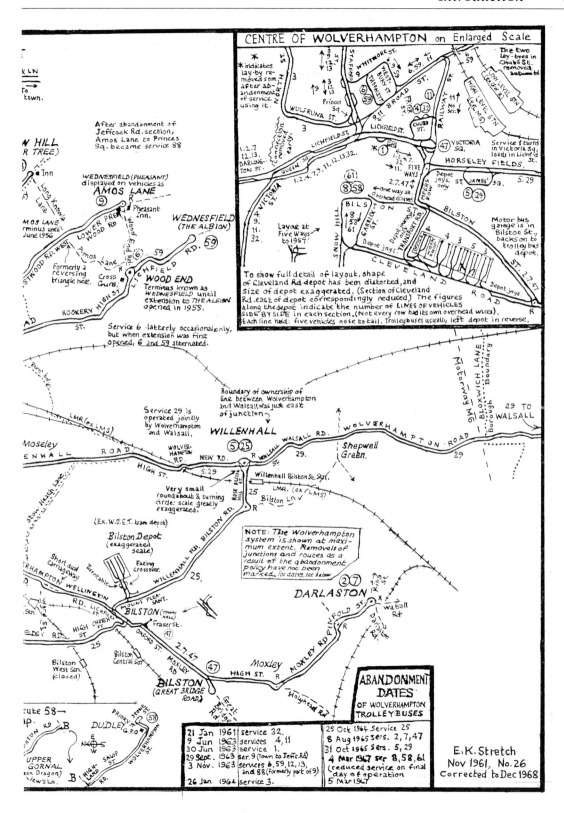

CENTRE OF WOLVERHAMPTON on Enlarged Scale

ABANDONMENT DATES OF WOLVERHAMPTON TROLLEYBUSES

21 Jan 1961	service 32.	25 Oct 1964	Service 25
9 Jun 1963	services 4, 11	8 Aug 1965	sers. 2, 7, 47
30 Jun 1963	service 1.	31 Oct 1965	sers. 5, 29
29 Sept. 1963	ser. 9 (Town to Jeffcock Rd)	4 Mar 1967	ser. 8, 58, 61
3 Nov. 1963	services 6, 59, 12, 13, and 88 (formerly part of 9)		(reduced service on final day of operation 5 Mar 1967)
26 Jan 1964	service 3.		

E.K. Stretch
Nov 1961, No. 26
Corrected to Dec 1968

introduced, locally produced Guy 'Arab' chassis, which had, like the COG5, been offered from its introduction with a Gardner diesel engine. The Daimlers were so successful that between 1935 and 1939 a total of 59 double-deck and single-deck COG5s were purchased, with the Loughborough bodybuilder Brush being favoured for all the double-deckers.

Wartime developments

The outbreak of the Second World War saw the bus fleet operating vehicles that were rarely more than seven years old, as compared to some of the trolleybus fleet, which were over 12 years old. Wartime restrictions on fuel supply, black-out regulations and the increased services to munitions factories such as Boulton Paul's aircraft factory at Pendeford, Guy Motors at Park Lane, Courtaulds factory at Dunstall Park and the Goodyear tyre factory on Stafford Road, meant a dramatic increase in the usage of vehicles, some of which were approaching the end of their economic lives. Consequently this placed a huge strain on the operating department of the Corporation.

The situation was somewhat relieved in September 1940 when 12 six-wheeled Sunbeam MS2 trolleybuses, with their two entrances and front and rear staircases, were borrowed from Bournemouth Corporation, but this was only a temporary respite in the quest for new vehicles. The bombing of Coventry on 14 November 1940 meant that the Daimler Motor Company was forced to re-locate from its destroyed Radford Works. Bus production was resumed in 1943 at the Courtaulds factory in Wolverhampton with the wartime CWG5 model, as was production of Daimler's famous military armoured Scout-Car. As well as all the other wartime production, the opening of the new Ordnance Factory to the north of the town at Featherstone on 6 June 1942 created a further strain on the Corporation bus fleet. Thus in 1943 Wolverhampton could boast two indigenous PSV manufacturers in Guy Motors and Sunbeam, with its badge-engineered Karrier trolleybus, as well as Daimler's temporary sojourn.

By the end of 1942 the Corporation had some 223 vehicles, of which only 198 could be housed in

the garages at Cleveland Road, Park Lane and Bilston. Although Wolverhampton received its first air-raid as late as 31 July 1942, and largely escaped the ravages that so badly affected nearby Birmingham and Coventry, the Transport Department adopted the policy of dispersing buses to sites around the town, such as West Park, which were agreed by the Regional Transport Committee. The need for extra vehicles became paramount, and in 1942 the Transport Department placed a bid with the MoWT for 12 trolleybuses. Despite all British wartime trolleybus production being based in the town, only six from the initial tranche of 50 Sunbeam/Karrier W4s were allocated to the under taking. These became 296-299/400-401 and arrived with Weymann MoWT-style bodies in July and August 1943. The withdrawal of many of the country services during the war meant that the newest Daimler COG5 single-deckers were rendered surplus to requirements and were duly sold during the latter part of the hostilities to more needy operators, namely Caerphilly UDC and nearby West Bromwich Corporation. By way of contrast, between 1943 and 1946 Wolverhampton was allocated another 32 Sunbeam W4 trolleybuses, four Guy 'Arab' Is, 20 Guy 'Arab' IIs and two Daimler CWD6s. These catered for the increase in traffic to and from the all-day shifts at the factories, but by the end of 1945 most of the pre-war trolleybus fleet, especially the six-wheelers, were well beyond the end of their economic lives.

Post-war changes

The trolleybus fleet was in dire need of replacement when in 1947, after an initial order for 22 Sunbeam W4s with post-war-styled Park Royal bodies had been received, an order was placed for 99 8-feet-wide trolleybuses. There were to be 49 Sunbeam F4s and 50 Guy BTs, the latter being destined to be the only BTs built after the war. All were to receive identical Park Royal 54-seater bodies, and this huge order effectively eliminated all the pre-war stock of trolleybuses, including the pre-war-styled trolleybuses delivered between 1940 and 1942, though they were quickly snapped up by Belfast Corporation, becoming their 235-245.

The immediate post-war motorbus investment was split between Daimler, following on from their dominance in the late 1930s in the Wolverhampton fleet, and Guy Motors. The latter's wartime success with its robust 'Arab' II model resulted in a large post-war order being placed by the Corporation for 40 Guy 'Arab' IIIs, 18 of which were bodied by Brush and 22 by Park Royal, both of whom had featured in the pre-war Wolverhampton body ordering policy. Thirty-seven Daimler CVG6s, all with Brush bodywork, were introduced into the fleet between 1948 and 1950, concurrently with the Guys. The last remnants of the pre-war single-deck fleet were also eliminated at this time when five Park Royal-bodied and five Guy-bodied Guy 'Arab' III single-deckers were delivered for use mainly, though not exclusively, on the rural services. Interestingly, Wolverhampton, although always parsimonious in its body specification, standardised its post-war orders by having them equipped with pre-select gearboxes, which although normal for the products manufactured by Daimler, were up to this time unheard of in the Guy 'Arab' range. By the time 'Arab' III production ended in 1954, only Belfast, Newport, South Shields, Sunderland and Wolverhampton Corporations had received the model with this type of gearbox, as well as a solitary bus, G436, which was given to London Transport for trial purposes, and the 100 'Arab' III Specials built for Birmingham City Transport in 1950 and 1951, which formed the basis of the later successful 'Arab' IV model (see David Harvey's chapter in *Classic Bus Year Book 8* for further details).

Throughout the mid-1950s the bus fleet remained fairly static, despite the increase in routes, particularly to the north of the town but also the services to Claverley, Wakeley Hill and Tettenhall Wood, which are found in this volume. A certain degree of upgrading took place at this time in order to maintain service levels in vehicles whose bodywork was prematurely beyond repair. Twenty of the wartime Guy 'Arab' IIs were rebodied by Roe between 1951 and 1952, while 16 of the earlier wartime trolleybuses were rebodied in 1952 by Park Royal in the by now somewhat old-fashioned style as the 434-455 batch, which had been constructed some five years earlier.

Between 1954 and 1957 some 33 Guy 'Arab'

IVs were delivered with bodies supplied by Metro-Cammell, Park Royal and Roe, all being normal half-cab, rear-entrance buses, and some of which were the last in the fleet to have Birmingham-style straight staircases. Nothing else was delivered to the Corporation between May 1957 and October 1958, when bus 19 (WUK 19) arrived. This vehicle set a new standard, being a 30-feet-long Guy 'Arab' IV with a forward-entrance, full-fronted 68-seat body. This layout, though reverting to half-cabs in later years, was to become the 'Wolverhampton standard' for the next eight years. Although the bodybuilder of 19, H. V. Burlingham, would not be used again, no fewer than 181 further 'Arab' IVs and the lower 'Arab' V were purchased, almost to the exclusion of every other double-decker type. These buses, bodied by MCCW, Park Royal and finally with the disastrous Strachan 'Paceline' body, spelled the end of the trolleybus system in Wolverhampton.

Trolleybus abandonment and the formation of the PTE

The first moves to close the trolleybus system were made in June 1957 when a report from Mr Addlesee suggested that 99 of the fleet of 153 trolleybuses were in need of replacement in the near future. The impending closure of the London Transport system effectively also drove a nail into the coffin of UK trolleybus operation. The usual 'anti-trolleybus' arguments were made in favour of abandonment. These included the lack of trolleybus manufacturers in late-1950s Britain, the extra cost of new trolleybuses over motorbuses, and the inflexibility of trolleybuses due to their fixed source of power. The early post-war mania to build ring roads around town and city centres inevitably meant that the overhead for trolleybuses had to be cut and, when completed, the power lines and the rest of the infrastructure were rarely replaced. In this respect, Wolverhampton was not unusual! The extensions into new housing estates beyond the existing route termini were rarely undertaken due to their expense, and since nationalisation the increased cost of electricity made the formerly cheap trolleybus something of an expensive millstone.

Despite the rebodying between 1958 and 1962 of the 38 Sunbeam W4s numbered between 418 and 455, the decision was made in March 1961 to gradually close down the Wolverhampton trolleybus system. The temporary closure of four routes in January 1961 in order to construct a pedestrian subway as part of Wolverhampton's inevitable ring road scheme presaged the first trolleybus route closure. On 22 May 1961 the Oxbarn Avenue (32) service was not re-instated, and the routes to Penn Fields (4) and Penn (11) were only revived for just over two years, both closing on 9 June 1963. The fourth of these temporarily suspended routes, the Jeffcock Road (9) service, was converted on 30 September 1963. The rest of the western trolleybus routes covered in this volume, to Finchfield (12) and Merry Hill (13), went soon afterwards, on 3 November 1963. The remainder of the system went over the next two years, leaving only the jointly operated route to Walsall (29), the Whitmore Reans to Darlaston route, and the long inter-urban 58 route to Dudley to survive into 1965. The Walsall and Willenhall trolleybus service was closed on 31 October 1965 because of the construction of the M6 motorway at Bentley; this was also the first Walsall Corporation service to close. This left the Dudley service to soldier on as the last trolleybus route operated by Wolverhampton Corporation. The original intention was to close the Dudley route in the spring of 1966, but delays in the delivery of the aforementioned Guy 'Arab' V double-deckers meant that the route had to be partially rewired in order to survive to its new date of closure. This was on Sunday 5 March 1967, which ironically was also the last day that the former GWR Low Level station was used by main-line services.

Within a year of the final trolleybus closure, the writing was on the wall for municipal operation in the town. The Labour Government of Harold Wilson produced a White Paper on its Transport Policy in 1966, and by 1968 the Transport Act proposed the setting up of new integrated transport bodies for six of the country's conurbations. The body for the West Midlands would be the West Midlands Passenger Transport Executive, and this was initiated on 1 April 1969, taking over the municipal operations of Birmingham, Walsall, West Bromwich and Wolverhampton. On 9 April 1969 the Wolverhampton Transport Committee held its last meeting, and on 22 September the final financial report of the undertaking was presented to the Town Council, showing a deficit of just over £200,000.

On 1 October 1969 the WMPTE took over the bus operation of services in Wolverhampton as well as those elsewhere in the West Midlands. For the public it meant the beginning of the end of the green and yellow buses that had served the town so well for more than 66 years.

Merry Hill and Finchfield

The trolleybus services to Finchfield (12A) and Merry Hill (13) are inexorably linked as they shared a common exit from the town centre through Chapel Ash, then along Merridale Road before splitting at Bantock Park. The two routes were opened on Monday 10 April 1933, together with the original Bradmore via Jeffcock Road service (9 north and 12 south). The opening day coincided with Francesco Agello setting a new world air speed record of 430.32mph in a Macchi-Castoldi 72 single-seater monoplane, but fortunately the new trolleybus services were just a little slower! The Finchfield 12A route became the south-westerly part of the cross-town service to Amos Lane, Wood End, as the 9 route, while the Merry Hill route was linked after 8 November 1937 with the Pear Tree, Cannock Road (9B) service on the north-eastern side of town. These two services to the north-east of Wolverhampton were also introduced on the same day, 21 March 1932, and both had a frequency of 15 minutes. On 13 June 1949, in order to simplify the route numbering system, which seemingly had become cumbersome with its additional suffix letters, the Finchfield Road service, together with a number of others, was renumbered, from 12A to 12. The Merry Hill route retained its original 13 number until both were closed on 3 November 1963.

The 12 and 13 services departed from outside the South Staffordshire Regiment Territorial Army Drill Hall in Stafford Street and went via Princes Square, Lichfield Street and Queen Square before descending Darlington Street and passing into Chapel Ash. At this complicated junction both routes turned into Merridale Road and for the first time entered a residential area. The town end of Merridale Road had been developed after the 1850s as far as the junction with Merridale Lane, where the Old Merridale Farm survived well into the 1920s, but by the time of the introduction of the trolleybuses it had ceased to be an agricultural enterprise.

Once beyond this junction the route crossed the valley of Graisley Brook and climbed up towards Merridale House and its grounds of 1734. This is now Bantock House; formerly the home of factory-owner Albert Bantock, it became a museum in April 1948 and displays some wonderful William Morris-styled late-19th-century 'Arts and Crafts' interiors. The two routes, having passed the abandoned lower section of Jeffcock Road near the General Cemetery, continued into Bradmore Road before reaching the Bradmore Village junction at Dead Lad's Grave, known locally for its ghostly apparitions! The area between Jeffcock Road and Birches Barn Road, opposite Bantock Park, was developed by the council in the 1920s as was the former north-western end of Stubbs Lane, now called Birches Barn Road. This was the only component of the four-way junction at Bradmore not to be served by trolleybuses.

At Bradmore the 12 route turned right alongside Bantock Park before reaching Finchfield Road West, where the trolleybuses left the open spaces of the park and turned left towards their terminus at the New Inn, which stood in the apex of the junction with Castlecroft Road. Here the trolleybuses left turned into Coppice Road, then reversed across the flow of traffic back into Castlecroft Road before crossing in front of the pub and drawing up at the inward pick-up stop outside a row of Victorian houses in Finchfield Road West. This was an extremely awkward manoeuvre, which must have been dreaded by the trolleybus crews. There were plans to extend the 12 route along Castlecroft Road, but this would have necessitated the construction of a new electricity sub-station to boost the power supply, and the plan never came to fruition.

From Bradmore the 13 route to Merry Hill continued straight on along Trysull Road, originally called Seisdon Road, through an area of housing built around the turn of the 20th century. On the corner of Trysull Road and Birches Barn Road is the Jacobean-styled Bradmore Arms public house, which dates from the 1920s. Once beyond Church Road, the route descended through an area of housing developed in the late 1920s and early 1930s towards the terminus at the Merry Hill public house and the Five Ways traffic island.

After the closure of both routes in 1963, the 12 bus route was extended along Finchfield Road, beyond the soon to be demolished New Inn (which was replaced by a traffic island!) and into White Oak Drive. The 43 bus route to Castlecroft followed the old trolleybus route except that it went directly into Finchfield Road rather than

going through Bradmore. It terminated at the County Borough boundary in Castlecroft Lane almost within sight of The Mermaid Inn at Wightwick on the Bridgnorth Road. The Merry Hill service remained largely unaltered until after the demise of the Corporation as a bus operator. In West Midlands PTE days this service, later having 500 added to the existing 13 number, was extended from Trysull Road into Coalway Road, then on to Warstones.

Below The 12 trolleybus service to Bradmore was originally opened on 10 April 1933 by way of Jeffcock Road, but was abandoned on 7 November 1937 when, on the following day, a new service, going by way of Chapel Ash and Merridale Road, replaced the previous Great Brickkiln Street and Rayleigh Road route. This section was incorporated into the later Jeffcock Road (9) service. The section of wiring along Jeffcock Road to Bradmore Road opposite Bantock Park remained in situ until after the Second World War, but was only used for trolleybus driver training. Standing in Stafford Street outside the Vine Hotel when working on the Bradmore 12 service in early 1937 is a rather antiquated seven-year-old six-wheeled trolleybus, 68 (UK 6768). This locally built Guy BTX was the second of a batch of four Dodson 61-seaters that entered service between May and September 1930. Strangely, these vehicles had six-bay bodies whereas the previous 62-66 batch were built to the more modern-looking five-bay construction, but the whole group was actually quite trail-blazing as they were the first trolleys in the Wolverhampton fleet to have low, one-step rear platforms. This can be seen by the very low position of the downstairs seating. The trolleybus is parked with its trolley-poles down while its crew stand behind it. *R. Wilson*

Opposite top The Merry Hill trolleybus route, numbered 13, had its town terminus in Stafford Street. Parked, driverless, outside the Territorial Army Regional Headquarters building in the late 1940s is one of the Park Royal-bodied Sunbeam

MF2s, 272 (BJW 172), which had entered service with the Corporation on 23 August 1938 and was one of three members of this batch of six not to be sold on to Southend-on-Sea Corporation for further use. After withdrawal on 30 November 1949 272 was destined to become a caravan in Shropshire, despite having been overhauled as recently as 6 April the same year! The slight panel damage just in front of the offside rear wheel arch rather spoils the otherwise apparently well-maintained bodywork, which by this time was about ten years old. It is in virtually its original livery style, although its dark, matt-grey-painted roof is a reminder of wartime camouflaging. The advertisement for 'Old Judge' Tea-'Tipps' is a reminder of just how many long-forgotten brands of the beverage have since disappeared. Having arrived in the town centre from Low Hill (Pear Tree) on the northern leg of its cross-town journey, the trolleybus will shortly load up and proceed into Princes Square before turning right into Lichfield Street. Behind the trolleybus is the three-gabled Wolverhampton Registry Office, whose Gothically styled portico has long looked down on many a confetti-throwing ceremony spilling on to Stafford Street. *R. Marshall*

Opposite middle Sunbeam W trolleybus 441 (EJW 441) stands in virtually the same position, working on the Merry Hill via Bradmore 13 service. As the trolleybus re-entered service on 18 June 1960 with the Charles Roe H32/28R body seen here, and the following vehicle, 463 (FJW 463), a Sunbeam F4 with an 8-feet-wide Park Royal body, was last used on 9 June 1963, this photograph must date to at least a year earlier. The latter vehicle was one of the trolleybuses to be officially withdrawn when the Penn and Penn Fields routes were abandoned on that date. Hidden by the leading vehicle is the Quick Snacks Bar, which was next to the impressive Victorian-built TA Drill Hall. 'If you want a treat, Try our 100% Hamburgers' was one of the snack bar's many window advertisements about this time, though one must imagine that its 'bread and butter' trade was perhaps BEST inside with a mug of tea (BEST being a gastronomic acronym for Bacon, Egg, Sausage and Tomato)! The cafe had previously been known as The Mayfair Cafe, but it changed its image in the late 1950s in an attempt to move into the 'coffee bar' era, obviously without much success. The crew are no doubt getting in a quick 'cuppa'. This part of Stafford Street, opposite what

today is part of the Wolverhampton University campus, has remained much the same in the intervening years, not falling foul of the redevelopment alongside the nearby Ring Road where it intersected Stafford Street (the A449) about 100 yards away. *C. W. Routh*

Bottom Guy Motors had to revert to a reasonably conventional front-engined double-deck chassis after its double debacle with the failure of the advanced 'Wulfrunian' model and the collapse of its investments in South Africa, which led to bankruptcy in October 1961. Having been taken over by Jaguar Cars in 1961, a new model was introduced in 1963; this was the 'Arab' V, which had a slightly lower chassis frame height than the previous, highly successful 'Arab' IV model. Guy only produced one 'Arab' V demonstrator, which was fitted with a Strachan H41/31F body. Unfortunately, Strachan's lack of recent experience in building double-deckers continued a somewhat broken line of short-lived and badly constructed 1940s and 1950s bodies of ghastly design. Having produced the peaked-roofed 'Paceline' prototype on 888 DUK, the fact that it failed to pass the tilt-test because it was top heavy quickly went around the industry and one can imagine potential buyers being distinctly put off from buying the 'Arab' V when this ugly pale-grey-liveried bus appeared. All, that is, except Wolverhampton! 888 DUK was demonstrated to the Corporation twice, first between December 1963 and February 1964, and again for just 19 days in February 1965. Here it is parked in Stafford Street outside the old TA Drill Hall during its first visit, having worked in from Low Hill on the recently abandoned 12 service. Strachan only ever received 'Paceline' double-decker orders from Wolverhampton, which bought two batches in 1965 and 1967 totalling 41 vehicles. Despite the excellent chassis, the pre-selector gearbox and the reliable Gardner 6LW engine, the cheaply built bodies were very quick to corrode and many achieved only five years' service before the dreaded 'tin-worm' got to them. Eleven of the buses enjoyed an after-life when they were sold to the China Bus Company of Hong Kong, where they were rebodied. 888 DUK was eventually sold to Harper Brothers of Heath Hayes in May 1966, surviving to be taken over by Midland Red on 7 September 1974, but being sold for scrap by early 1975. *A. B. Cross*

Top During the last year of municipal bus operation, travelling out of Stafford Street, with the TA Drill Hall and Registry Office behind it, is 145 (145 DDA). A Guy 'Arab' V, it was powered by a Gardner 6LW engine, and was one of 25 Park Royal forward-entrance 72-seaters. This 'Arab' V/ Park Royal combination was unique; indeed, these buses were the last Guys ever to be bodied by Park Royal, and 145, Wolverhampton's penultimate example, was delivered in February 1964. It is working on the 12 service to Finchfield, crossing into Princes Square with Broad Street on the right, and passing The Vine Hotel on the corner. The Morris Minor 1000 van behind it was registered in Birmingham in 1968 and is being followed by a Triumph Herald, while a Hillman Imp travels out of town into Stafford Street. In the distance on the right is Whitmore Street, which in trolleybus days was used as the terminus of the westbound Jeffcock Road service. *A. D. Broughall*

Middle Waiting in Railway Street on 6 June 1949, alongside the Coal and Brick Wharf when working on the 43 service to Castlecroft, is one of Wolverhampton Corporation's last pre-war single-deckers, 357 (BUK 557), a Daimler COG5/40 dating from 1939. Unusually for a West Midlands operator, these buses had stylish B34R bodies built by John Beadle, a bodybuilder based in Rochester, Kent. They were only to see 11 years' service before being replaced in March 1950 by ten Guy 'Arab' III single-deckers, and were typical of the pre-war Wolverhampton Corporation bus fleet, being equipped with EKO destination blinds that had the same lettering style as that used by neighbouring Birmingham Corporation. The 43

service was introduced in February 1949 as an extension of the 12 trolleybus route into the Castlecroft housing estate, and for its first year it was exclusively operated by single-deckers. The lightly loaded 43 service is now operated by Travel West Midlands, which used Metrobus double-deckers for a number of years to increase the service frequency from 20 to 10 minutes. The route is now numbered 543 by TWM, and uses the latest low-floor Optare XL single-deckers, whose capacity, at 33, is one less than the Daimler single-decker of 50 years earlier. *D. R. Harvey collection*

Opposite bottom On leaving Railway Street, the 43 service to Castlecroft crossed Victoria Square on its way to its westerly exit from the town via Lichfield Street. Towering over Railway Street on the corner of Victoria Square is the Prince Albert Hotel, while as if acting as a protective stockade around two sides of the square are imposing advertising hoardings. Above the trolleybus on the right is an advertisement for EMVA Cream, a 'British' sherry. The writer thought as a child that somewhere in Britain was an area devoted to viticulture, and it came as a shock to realise that this beautiful product of the Jerez region of Spain was in fact imported into Britain in a bulk tanker by Empire Wine Vaults (hence EMVA) of Stirchley, Birmingham, and bottled by them! The trolleybus beneath the advertisement is 413 (DJW 943), a Sunbeam W4 chassis of May 1945 that was numerically only the 146th to be built. It is carrying its second Park Royal body, which in this case was fitted in May 1952. Travelling through Victoria Square is 510 (FJW 510), a Daimler CVG6 with a Brush 54-seater body, which is manoeuvring around the island in front of the Victoria Hotel. It is working on the 43 service to Castlecroft, its emptiness readily demonstrating why single-deckers were best suited to this route, although it has yet to reach its main picking-up points in Queen Square and Darlington Street. Following the bus is a forward-control Ford Thames 15cwt van. This was the model that pre-dated the more famous Transit van, but which in its day, with its semi-underfloor engine, revolutionised the light van market. Parked in the centre of Victoria Square is a Standard Vanguard Phase I, while next to it is an Austin FX3 taxi-cab of a type more associated with London. *R. F. Mack*

Above right Passing through Princes Square on the 12 service to Finchfield is one of the Bournemouth Corporation trolleybuses that seemed to be marooned in Wolverhampton for *years*! It is the awful winter of 1946-47, which, after several bad blizzards before the end of the year, culminated in a snowstorm that began across the country on 24 January 1947 and continued throughout February and into March. It was the worst snowfall since a series of severe winters between 1878 and 1897, while it considerably eclipsed the bad weather of January 1940. It was in September 1940 that Wolverhampton Corporation was able to hire 12 Bournemouth trolleybuses at a rate of £240 per vehicle per year. This was intended to relieve the problem of the late delivery of the last ten Sunbeam MS2s, which, though ordered in 1940, did not all arrive until April 1942. The Bournemouth Corporation vehicles were all six-wheeled Sunbeam MS2s of a type that Wolverhampton already operated; the big difference was that their Park Royal bodies were only 56-seaters and were equipped with a front as well as the normal rear staircase. There was also an additional front exit protected by a set of two-leaf jack-knife doors, a feature of all Bournemouth's trolleybuses. While it posed little problems for Newcastle Corporation, whose indigenous trolleybuses were of a layout identical to the nine it hired, elsewhere, where the Bournemouth Sunbeams operated, in London, Llanelly, South Shields, Walsall and here in Wolverhampton, only the rear open back platform was used.

This example, 137 (BEL 822), a 1935-built MS2, arrived in Wolverhampton on 3 October 1940 when the Battle of Britain was still taking place, and was one of the last to leave when it was returned to the Hampshire resort, refurbished and repainted, on 1 November 1948. The movement of trolleybuses from the South Coast towns of Bournemouth, Brighton, Hastings and Portsmouth served several purposes, as that part of England was designated a Prohibited Area due to the proximity of Occupied France. With the distinct possibility of Hitler's 'Operation Sea Lion' invasion, these towns not only had a surplus of vehicles but also needed to disperse them to other parts of the country, which provided industrial towns such as Newcastle, South Shields and Wolverhampton with much-needed extra trolleybuses. For example, during the Second World War many of Wolverhampton's factories were working three eight-hour shifts every day, and there was a need for transport round the clock. Fortunately Wolverhampton escaped the devastating bombing raids that caused such havoc and loss of life in nearby industrialised Birmingham and Coventry.

The trolleybus is passing in front of W. Snape's gentlemen's outfitters shop on the west corner of Princes Square. Years before, Snape's premises had belonged to another bespoke tailor called Price Lewis, which occupied the impressive Victorian premises throughout the first quarter of the century, and Snapes seemed somehow to be a logical successor. These buildings were constructed for the Royal London Mutual Insurance Company in 1902 to the designs of Essex, Nicol and Goodman. *A. Evans*

Below Turning across Princes Square from Stafford Street in 1961 is one of the 1952 Park Royal-rebodied wartime Sunbeam W4s, 404 (DJW 904). At this point the driver will be undertaking a series of foot manoeuvres on the left-foot throttle that would have done justice to Fred Astaire, accelerating and coasting as he heaves his heavy-steering charge through the plethora of overhead wiring, 'frogs' and points as he turns right into the Art Gallery end of Lichfield Street. Personal experience has shown that trolleybus driving is a most difficult art, and one false move leads to sudden dewirement! Behind the trolleybus and the passing Standard 10 saloon is a four-storey block of late-Victorian shops, including Frames Tours, which also double as a British Railways booking agency. The traffic lights to the right of the Merry Hill-bound trolleybus were the first set of electrically operated traffic lights to be installed in Britain; they were originally suspended from wires above the junction and came into use on Saturday 5 November 1927. By 1961 they are fixed to a traction pole, which has also acquired a record number of attachments, including not only the four-way traffic lights at eye-level, but also two span arms for the overhead and six RAC road signs! *J. C. Brown*

Opposite above Facing Cleveland Street is the Wulfrun Centre, and parked outside when working on the 35 service is 18 (SUK 18), a Meadows-powered Guy 'Arab' IV fitted with a Metro-Cammell H33/27R body. The Wulfrun Centre was unusually linked to Cleveland Street by a 'travelator', one of the first moving pavements of a sort more usually associated with international airports. The Wulfrun Centre was built as a joint venture by Wolverhampton Corporation and the Hammerson Group between 1966 and 1969 to the designs of Bernard Engle & Son. It replaced many old, small, traditional shops, but was able to accommodate some of the

biggest national retail chains such as the Early Learning Centre and Argos. While it was a success and separated pedestrians from traffic with its open precincts, paved arcades and walkways, its concrete-faced upper floors, masking the upper-storey car parks, soon began to look very dated. In 1994 the Centre was in dire need of refurbishment, and with the existing owners being unable to support any of the necessary work, it sold to London & Cambridge Properties, who drew up plans similar to those that had been realised in the Cornbow Centre in Halesowen, the Churchill Centre in Dudley and the Crown Centre in Stourbridge, whereby the precincts were enclosed, allowing comfortable 'weather-free' shopping. *D. R. Harvey collection*

Below right With the trolleybus wires gone and the remaining traction poles, some even having remnants of the span wires, standing forlornly along Darlington Street, this part of the town centre doesn't seem to have got used to not having the silent service! This once thriving shopping street is in terminal decline in June 1964 as Guy 'Arab' IV 50 (4050 JW), working on the 43 service to Castlecroft, passes the entrance of Art Street in the foreground. On the left are some of the original mid-19th-century buildings that would be demolished in the next two years to make way for the second stage of the ring road, which included the huge Chapel Ash traffic island. Compulsory purchase orders anywhere are the kiss of death to trading, and this lower part of the street suffered from 'planning blight' for a number of years. Behind the bus is the five-storey Clarence House office block, and beyond that the traffic lights at Waterloo Road. To the nearside of the full-fronted double-decker is a 1962-registered MG 1100, while facing uphill towards the town is a Ford Cortina Super 118E dating from August 1963. *S. R. Dewey*

Above Travelling down Darlington Street on 1 June 1963, working on the 12 route to Finchfield, is Park Royal-bodied 8-feet-wide trolleybus 470 (FJW 470), one of the 1948 batch of Sunbeam F4s that entered service on 23 October of that year. Although this trolleybus route was abandoned on 3 November 1963, this trolleybus, which looks in good quite condition with its white-painted steering wheel to denote one of these wider vehicles, would in fact run for the last time on 9 June, when the important Penn Road trolleybus service was closed, resulting in the withdrawal of some 15 vehicles. To the right are the former premises of the horse-tram depot, which dated from 1878 and was opened on 1 May of that year on the line of the town's first horse-tram route. This was operated by the Wolverhampton Tramway Company, which went from Queen Square to Newbridge and survived until the route was electrified by the Corporation. The depot was closed during the same year as superfluous to requirements, and the property was subsequently sold to the Corporation's Water Department. Parked outside the old depot is a Vauxhall Victor FB four-door saloon and a Hillman Minx Series IIIB. In the distance are the twin domes of the Wesleyan Methodist Chapel on the corner of School Street. Between this church and the tram depot is a Roe-bodied Sunbeam W4 trolleybus and a Guy 'Arab' IV, fitted with a full-front style of Metro-Cammell body. Travelling into the town centre, just beyond the parked black Austin Cambridge A55, is an early Triumph Spitfire, while beyond that are two further trolleybuses. *J. Hughes*

Below The cross-town 26 service was the nearest thing the Corporation ever got to a more traditional Inner Circle service. Starting from Kempthorne Avenue, Low Hill, on the north side of the town, it proceeded along Bushbury Lane before meandering into the edge of Whitmore Reans and

New Hampton Road. It then skirted the Molineux football ground and, on reaching Chapel Ash, crossed the other Darlington Street trolleybus and bus routes, including the Merry Hill and Finchfield routes, by way of Salop Street. It then went on to Goldthorn Park by way of Ednam Road. Just after the take-over of Wolverhampton Corporation by the WMPTE, Metro-Cammell 'Orion'-bodied Guy 'Arab' IV 583 (KJW 583), which entered service in June 1954, travels along Ednam Road on the Goldthorn Park Estate. It is a sunny day in the summer of 1970 and the bus is carrying 'West Midlands' Fablon fleet-name stickers instead of the municipal crests. This Birmingham-style 'New Look'-fronted double-decker would stay in service until 1971, but would never receive the light blue and cream livery of the PTE. *D. R. Harvey collection*

Right In 1948, when virtually new, 508 (FJW 508), a Brush-bodied Daimler CVG6, stands in Himley Crescent, the terminus of the Goldthorn Park (26) service, which although instigated before the Second World War, really only came into its own in the early post-war period when the estate was completed. The bus is about to reverse out into Ednam Road, and behind it are the wide open spaces of the undeveloped land along that road. When this housing development was built it was in Sedgley UDC, but in 1966 the Goldthorn Park Estate came under the control of Wolverhampton. The picture reveals that this first batch of post-war Daimler CVG6s was delivered with black-painted radiators rather than the more normal chromed variety. In the years after the Second

World War, with a shortage of chrome, many bus chassis manufacturers, including Daimler, supplied buses with fleet-colour-painted radiators. Many municipalities continued to favour this option even though chrome became available by the end of the 1940s. An order for 98 exposed-radiator CVG6s for Belfast Corporation was completed as late as 1954 and all but two had black-painted radiators. 508 is painted in the extremely smart post-war livery of green lower panels and yellow mid and upper panels, broken with two thin black bands. The dark grey roof is a throwback to wartime camouflaging. *R. Hannay*

Below Sunbeam W4 415 (DUK 15) turns out of Merridale Road in front of a Ford Anglia 105E and crosses into

Chapel Ash, with the 'trolleybus-less' Compton Road immediately behind it along which the disappearing ambulance is travelling. This Park Royal-rebodied trolleybus is working into Wolverhampton on the 12 service from Finchfield and has the destination blind set for the Low Hill (Pear Tree) terminus on the north-east side of the town. To the right and beyond the Bentley S1 saloon, with the registration DA 90, is the lovely row of Regency terraced houses that line Tettenhall Road. Just visible is a trolleybus working into the town on the 1 route from Tettenhall. The building on the corner of Tettenhall Road and Compton Road is Westbourne Place, which dates from the 1820s, and by 18 August 1962 is being used by Small's School of Motoring. *J. C. Brown*

Opposite page With the tower of the Presbyterian Church dominating the skyline in Merridale Road, Park Royal-bodied Sunbeam W4 455 (EJW 455) has just left Chapel Ash working on the 12 route to Finchfield. This trolleybus entered service on 24 January 1948 and was the last of this model to be delivered to the Corporation. It also had the distinction of being Wolverhampton's only trolleybus to be equipped with saloon heaters. It has just passed The Manse on the corner of Oak Drive, home of the minister of the Presbyterian Church. Beyond the church is a distant Atkinson's-owned public house on the corner of Lord Street, whose asymmetrical window arrangement suggests an alteration to avoid payment in the 18th century. Following the trolleybus is a 1954-registered short-wheelbase Land Rover, a Commer QX four-wheeled lorry fitted with the unconventional Rootes three-cylinder horizontal two-stroke diesel engine, and a DKW 1000 four-seater coupé, which strangely enough is also powered by a two-stroke engine, only this time a much smaller 980cc example. Towering above the distant Chapel Ash is Banks's Park Brewery in Bath Road.

The 1930s terrace of shops still stands on Merridale Road next door to the secluded house and gardens known as The Oaks. This large, elegant house dates from 1830 and was owned by John Marston, a successful industrialist who branched out from his original japanning industry into the fashionable production of 'safety' cycles. In 1887 he produced the Sunbeam Safety Cycle, and, with his son Charles, quickly graduated to the production of motorcycles and eventually, in 1901, motorcars. These were sold under the name of Sunbeam, a marque that would be devalued after it was sold to the Rootes Group in 1935. In the 1950s The Oaks was sold and became the head office of the Wolverhampton Water Undertaking, remaining as such until it was taken into the ownership of the Severn-Trent Water Authority. On 17 July 2000 Travel West Midlands Metrobus Mk II 2441 (NOA 441X) leaves the bus stop in Merridale Road when working on the 513 service. Behind the bus is the Rover car showroom that replaced the Manse and the Presbyterian Church. The pub on the corner of Lord Street has long since closed. *D. R. Harvey collection/D. R. Harvey*

Below The houses lining the outer section of Merridale Road dated from the post-1860s period and consisted of a mixture of large bay-windowed terraced villas, taking the limit of mid-Victorian development out to the junction with Merridale Lane and Old Merridale Farm, barely half a mile from the Chapel Ash junction. The farm was removed when the 1920s housing behind the traffic island was built, but a glimpse of this location in the last decade of the 19th century would have revealed gently rolling farmland stretching away towards the nearby Graisley Brook valley. Only the white-faced house on the corner of Merridale Road on the extreme right and the much earlier premises of the Merridale Paint Company, formerly part of Old Merridale Farm, were in existence at that time. Some 60 years on, on 18 August 1962, a two-tone Austin A40 Farina two-door saloon appears to be involved in a race around the Merridale Lane traffic island with a black Ford Consul EOTA. In front of Timken Stockists Ltd – it should have been a greengrocer or a butcher in such premises – is a Hillman Minx Series IIIB, which is turning behind the trolleybus. The bus is rebodied Sunbeam W4 420 (DUK 820) of 1946, which re-entered service with its new Roe H32/28R body on 29 December 1958, and is working on 13 route from Merry Hill to Low Hill (Pear Tree). These attractive bodies by the Leeds-based bodybuilder were produced, with minor differences, for Ashton, Maidstone and Doncaster Corporations as well as the Teesside Railless Traction Board based at North Ormsby. The capital expenditure on rebodying these wartime trolleybuses might have been difficult to justify, as the process, which started in 1958 and eventually involved 38 new bodies, served only to keep the system operational until 1967. This example was to work for just under seven years in this new guise, being withdrawn on 31 October 1965 when the joint service to Walsall closed. *J. C. Brown*

Below The valley of Graisley Brook was only developed for housing during the 1950s when the Merridale Court flats were built on the south-eastern side of Merridale Road; these are on the right where the man with the ladder is undertaking some property maintenance on this sunny Tuesday afternoon, 4 August 1962. If his work at the flats was warm, then pity the poor driver of trolleybus 466 (FJW 466) in his cab as he heaves his heavy-steering charge along the 12 route to Finchfield via Bradmore Road. The sliding cab door was a boon to the driver in hot weather as he could drive with it open. This Park Royal-bodied Sunbeam F4 entered service on 20 October 1948 and would survive until the last day of July 1965. As it accelerates up the tree-lined hill towards the Finchfield Road junction at Bantock Park, it is being followed by a couple of Morris Minor 1000s. *J. C. Brown*

Opposite above As the Finchfield and Merry Hill trolleybuses travelled along Bradmore Road towards the town centre they passed Bantock Park on their left. On the opposite side of Bradmore Road, the triangular site at the Jeffcock Road junction on the left is graced with some lovely mid-19th-century villas, originally known as Beaumont Terrace. A traction pole on the corner of Jeffcock Road is a reminder of when trolleybuses briefly used this bottom end of the road; the section from Bradmore Road to Jeffcock Road, which had only been opened in April 1933, closed on 7 November 1937, but the original wiring, which had a 1ft 6in spacing, was left in situ until 1945. The speeding trolleybus, Park Royal-bodied Guy BT 641 (FJW 641), is about to enter Merridale Road as it travels towards Chapel Ash. In Bantock Park is the delightful Bantock House, visible through the trees just in front of the trolleybus. Originally built as Merridale Farm, the rear of the present house dates from about 1734, while the classically styled frontage is at least 70 years newer. Merridale House was purchased by local industrialist Thomas Bantock in 1867. Renamed Bantock House, his eldest son, Albert Baldwin Bantock, began a large refurbishment using interiors inspired by William Morris's 'Arts and Crafts' movement. A. B. Bantock became an alderman and was Mayor of Wolverhampton in 1905-6, 1906-7 and 1914-15. After his death in 1937 the house was bequeathed to the Corporation, but was not opened to the public until 22 April 1948 due to military requisition during the Second World War. Its interior is graced with Delft-tiled fireplaces, wood-panelled main entrance hall and ground-floor rooms, and moulded ceilings. *J. C. Brown*

Below right Most of the housing opposite Bantock Park in Bradmore Road was municipal property dating from either 1920 or 1921 and formed part of the Corporation's housing estate built near the site of the old Merridale Brick Works. Bradmore Road was served by a number of Corporation-operated services; as well as the trolleybus services to Finchfield and Merry Hill, there was also the 35 bus service to Warstones and the country bus services to Trysull, Halfpenny Green, Bobbington and Claverley. Working on the 13 Merry Hill service is Wolverhampton Corporation's last pre-war trolleybus, 281 (BJW 181), a Guy BT with an attractive Roe H29/25R body, fitted with that company's patented staircase, which entered service on 17 September 1938 in an all-over green livery. The pre-war heavy-steering Guy BT trolleybuses were slightly less powerful than the contemporary Sunbeam MF2s; they had EEC 75hp motors, whereas 'the opposition' were equipped with Metro-Vickers 80hp motors. Following the trolleybus, on the way out of town, is wartime Guy 'Arab' I 360 (DJW 560), the first 'utility' Park Royal-bodied bus in the fleet, which, unlike the trolleybus, is painted in the more usual mainly primrose livery. The trolleybus would be withdrawn on the last day of November 1949 when only 11 years old, whereas 360 would survive in its original state until 1957. *S. N. J. White*

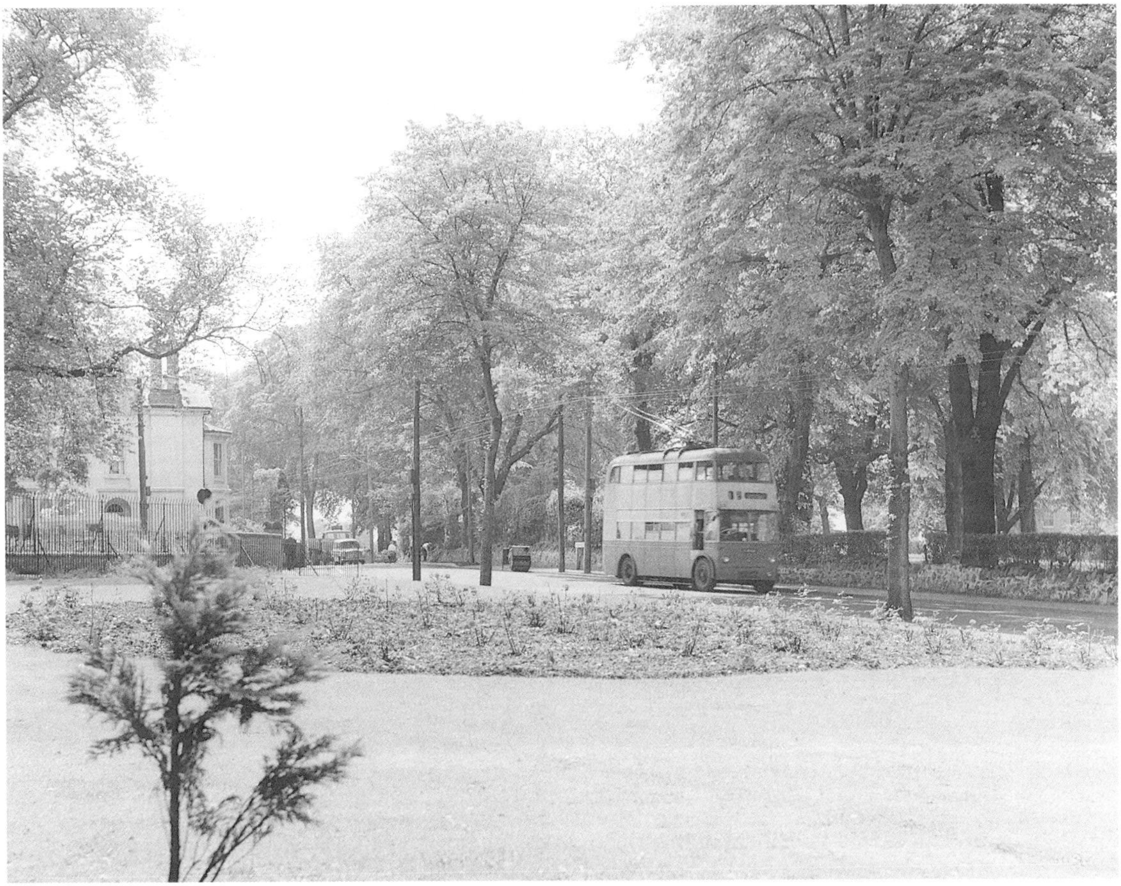

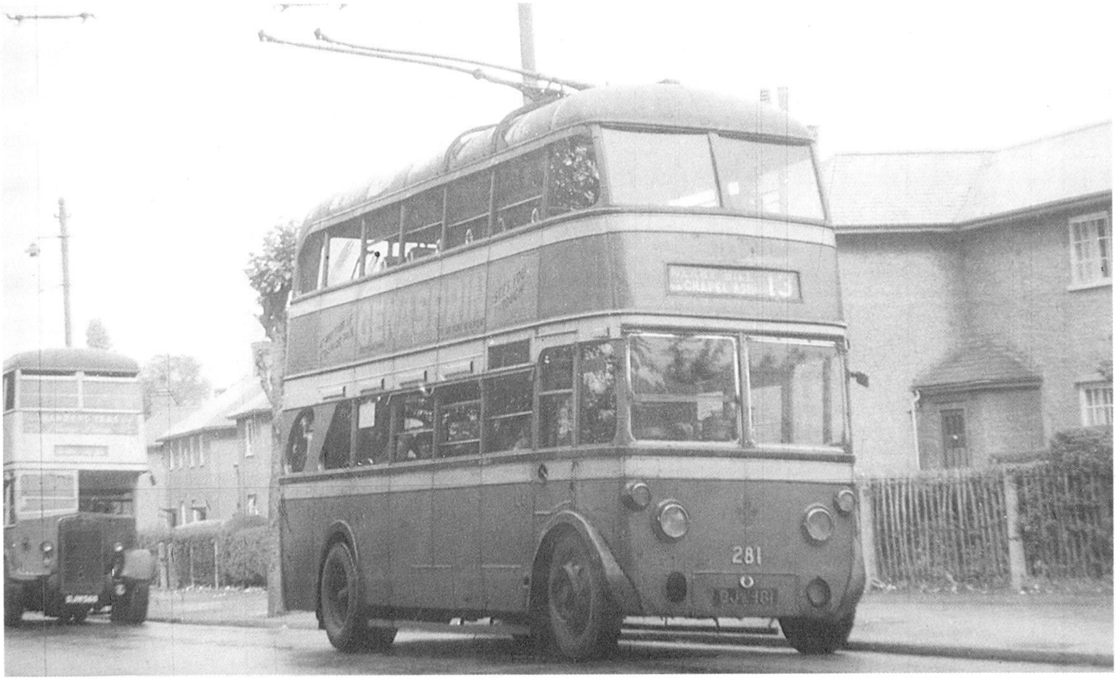
281

This page Approaching the Broad Lane-Birches Barn Road junction is one of the 95hp Metro-Vickers-powered, Park Royal-bodied Sunbeam F4s, 473 (FJW 473), which entered service on 9 October 1948. It is travelling along Bradmore Road when working on the 13 service in the summer of 1961. It has passed the distant Bantock House Museum, which can be seen through the trees in the centre of the photograph, and is approaching the point where the 12 and 13 trolleybus services diverged. On the right is Birches Barn Road, which led to the terminus of the Penn Fields (4) route at Lea Road about half a mile away, while the 12 service used Broad Lane on the left and followed the boundary of Bantock Park; 473 will, however, travel straight across the junction into Trysull Road.

Having just left the bus stop in Bradmore Road on 17 July 2000 is 3120 (G120 FJW), one of the last MCW 'Metrobus' Mk IIs delivered to the then West Midlands Travel in November 1989. It is about to cross the by now traffic-light-controlled junction into Trysull Road. The passing years have seen the trees around Bantock Park grow considerably, somewhat hiding the lovely Bantock House. The Metrobus is being used on the successor to the old 13 trolleybus route, which in common with all the Wolverhampton Corporation service numbers had 500 added to the old route number; on reaching the old trolleybus terminus at Merry Hill the 513 service will turn back towards Warstones. The road sign on the right, in Birches Barn Road, shows that Penn is only 1½ miles away, while to the left, on the corner of Broad Lane, from where the silver Honda car is emerging, Compton is a similar distance away. *J. C. Brown/ D. R. Harvey*

Opposite top A cyclist pedals his delivery bicycle into Broad Lane adjacent to a service road that provides access to a block of 1930s shops. He appears unaware of the somewhat weather-beaten trolleybus turning behind him from Bradmore Road. The driver of trolleybus 418 (DUK 18) has cleared the overhead junction over

which he has just accelerated at about 5mph; the power has actuated a 'frog' on the overhead to enable the trolleybus to turn off the 'main-line' route straight on into Trysull Road, and instead turn right into Broad Lane. Sunbeam W4 418, rebodied by Charles Roe and re-entering service in June 1959, is seen undertaking this manoeuvre on 18 November 1961, some 12 months before it would receive its last repaint. It is working on the Finchfield 12 service, which had almost another two years of operational life in front of it before its conversion to motorbuses. Beyond the litter bin in the right foreground is a Bedford CA van; this is the long-wheelbase version, and can be identified by the extra-long sliding cab doors. *J. C. Brown*

Middle Having unloaded at the top of Oxbarn Avenue near the junction of Warstones Road, bus 579 (KJW 579) is working on the 35 motorbus service. It appears to be brand new, judging by the still shiny state of its tyres, which would date the photograph to not long after June 1954, when the bus entered service. Behind the bus are the early post-war council houses that were also served by the nearby Coalway Road 32 trolleybus service. The bus, a Guy 'Arab' IV fitted with a Metro-Cammell H30/26R 'Orion' body, will travel the mile or so to the terminus in Warstones Road at Spring Hill Lane, which in turn was within a few hundred yards of the Penn trolleybus service. *J. C. Brown*

Bottom An unidentified Park Royal-bodied trolleybus is working on the Merry Hill (13) route and is travelling along Trysull Road away from the Bradmore Road junction towards the terminus about three-quarters of a mile away. The family of three are walking past the Bradmore Arms public house, which closed in early 2002, on the forecourt of which is parked an early post-war Vauxhall Wyvern LI model, dating from between 1948 and 1951, between which years some 55,409 of this 1442cc column-gearchange car were produced. On the far corner of Star Street is Butler's Star Stores, housed in a late-19th-century building, which has since been replaced by modern premises including the Bradmore Fryer fish and chip shop. The traction poles in Trysull Road were set only on the eastern side of the road at this point and the bracket arms carried both sets of running wires. *S. Ferrier*

Left Heading towards Wolverhampton on the 13 service from Merry Hill is Sunbeam W4 trolleybus 406 (DJW 906), rebodied by Park Royal in March 1952. It is passing Marnel Drive in Trysull Road, about halfway between Bantock Park and the Five Ways island terminus, while travelling towards Merry Hill is a Bedford CA van. The trolleybus is about to pass beneath the thick feeder cables providing the next section of overhead with power, which in Wolverhampton was rated at 550V. It will coast beneath this section of the overhead as accelerating would blow the circuit breakers in the cab, temporarily disabling the vehicle. The rows of 1920s houses in Trysull Road are interrupted by two shops on the right. *J. C. Brown*

Below left The outer part of the Merry Hill route along Trysull Road saw a scattering of Victorian properties gradually giving way to the inter-war housing of Wolverhampton's suburbia. The two men on the right are running to get to the bus stop before the rapidly approaching rebodied Sunbeam W4 trolleybus. Having left the Five Ways terminus, it is passing the junction with New Street on the left, a short road through to Coalway Road. This outward section of the trolleybus route had traction poles on both sides of the road, with the overhead carried on span wires. Even at this late stage of the system, in the summer of 1962, the overhead seems in remarkably good order, being taut and not sagging. The trolleybus is 443 (EJW 443), which received a new Roe body in February 1962, having been off the road for exactly 12 months. *S. Ferrier*

This page The terminus of the Merry Hill trolleybus route was at the Five Ways island, where the vehicles did a 360-degree turn back into Trysull Road, to load up outside the mock-Elizabethan Merry Hill public house. Clustered on the Coalway Road side of the junction are a row of 1930s shops, while behind the open space in the foreground, between Finchfield Lane and the unusually spelt Bhylls Lane, are another collection of local shops. In the late 1950s these small suburban shops were able to supply the local community with its regular, everyday household requirements. Soon, however, the 'bubble would burst', caused in no little way by the availability of small, mass-produced motorcars, such as the 1955 Standard 8 glimpsed coming out of Coalway Road on the extreme left. Once the car came within the financial means of householders, the role of public transport in providing a cheap service mainly for workers, schoolchildren and people going on 'shopping expeditions to town' changed and declined. With it went the small shops, as by the end of the 1960s the pattern of retailing had also begun to alter with the advent of supermarket shopping. Sunbeam W trolleybus 444 (EJW 444), delivered in December 1947 and still with its original 54-seater Park Royal, straight-staircase body, negotiates the Five Ways island in about 1958. The road to the right is Langley Road, which continues to the nearby countryside, taking the 18, 48 and 54 motorbus routes to the villages of the Smestow Valley and beyond.

In the intervening 40-odd years surprisingly little in the area has changed. The most noticeable alteration is the construction of three blocks of 15-storey flats that tower over the area. Somehow the sheer size of these 'houses in the sky' seems out of scale with the neat row of shops beneath them. Those behind the silver BMW 5 Series saloon have changed more subtly over the years and now contain an 'open all hours' 'convenience store', while the block beneath the flats has in it a butcher and Merry Hill's Post Office. Behind the photographer is a florist and greengrocer as well as a Chinese take-away. In the distance, on 17 July 2000, a Mark II MCW 'Metrobus' double-decker of Travel West Midlands passes the St Joseph of Arimathea Church as it disappears along Coalway Road on its way to Warstones on the 513 service. *J. Hughes collection/D. R. Harvey*

Top Eight-foot-wide, Park Royal-bodied Sunbeam F4 472 (FJW 472) turns round the Five Ways island. It is empty, having disgorged its passengers at the Trysull Road 13 trolleybus route terminus, and is about to turn back into Trysull Road to load up outside the Merry Hill public house. In the distance, to the left of the trolleybus, is Langley Road, while coming out of Bhylls Lane is a Vauxhall Victor Series F Mark II. Standing on the forecourt of the shops between Finchfield Lane and Bhylls Lane are two lady shoppers, while careful examination reveal the extended sunblind of the greengrocer's shop. The trolleybus driver has been extremely efficient as he has already altered the destination blind to read 'LOW HILL (PEAR TREE)' before he has even reached the inbound picking-up stop. *J. Hughes collection*

Middle The first day of December 1973 looks somewhat cold, judging by the fur coat being worn by the lady about to climb aboard the bus at the terminus of the 18 route. The bus is 123 (123 DDA), a 1964 Guy 'Arab' V with a Park Royal H41/31F body, and is outside the King's Arms public house and opposite All Saints Parish Church, Claverley. It will proceed through the village, passing the Crown and the Plough public houses as well as many of the half-timbered buildings that grace Claverley, before going on to Trysull and Halfpenny Green. The buses came into the town by way of Trysull Road and Merry Hill, following in part the 13 trolleybus route. Once a Great Western Railway bus service, it was extended as the 18A to reach Claverley by 2 May 1925. For many years it warranted only a single-decker, but from the mid-1950s onwards double-deckers were used because of the extra traffic being generated beyond the Merry Hill trolleybus terminus. *R. Smith*

Bottom Meanwhile, back at Bantock Park on the 12 route, Sunbeam W4 trolleybus 451 (EJW 451), which had re-entered service with its new Charles Roe H32/28R body on 11 April 1961, is waiting at the bus stop in Broad Lane about a third of the way between Finchfield Road and Bradmore Road as it travels on its way into the town centre on 18 November 1961. It is a bleak-looking afternoon, with the bare branches of the birch trees standing starkly against the cloud-laden sky; even Bantock Park, where children are kicking a football about, usually an inviting area of greenery, looks mean, cold and deserted. Through this winter's scene passes the trolleybus, being overtaken by a 1960 locally registered Morris Minor 1000, while travelling towards Finchfield Road is an Austin A55 van. *J. C. Brown*

Above Sunbeam W4 402 (DJW 902) was numerically the first of Wolverhampton's wartime trolleybuses to receive a new body. It had originally entered service with a Park Royal 'utility' body on 16 December 1944, and was rebodied in February 1952 with another Park Royal product of the same type that had been supplied on the new 434-455 batch of vehicles delivered to the Corporation four years earlier, between March 1947 and January 1948. It was withdrawn after the closure of the Penn and Penn Fields trolleybus services in 1963, but on 8 August 1962 it is reversing out of the Coppice Road stub section of wiring into Castlecroft Road at the terminus of the Finchfield 12 service. This was the only place on the Wolverhampton system where trolleybuses undertook such an extremely awkward manoeuvre, which must have been dreaded by the drivers when they saw that they had been rostered for 'a turn on the 12'. Between Castlecroft Road, used by the 43 motorbus service, and Finchfield Road West on the right is the Victorian-built Butler's-brewery owned New Inn public house. The elderly gentlemen on the right is standing at the pick-up stop in Finchfield Road West alongside which the trolleybus will eventually stop. *J. C. Brown*

Right On 10 August 1960 Sunbeam W 403 (DJW 903) stands in the short dead-end stub of wiring in Coppice Road into which empty trolleybuses turned. The conductor, with warning whistle in mouth, is standing in

Castlecroft Road with the white-walled New Inn public house behind him, and will 'watch the driver back' as the trolleybus slowly reverses past the large tree with the small stone wall around its base. It might have been easier had the overhead been arranged to allow trolleybuses to reverse into Coppice Road, but presumably this was not done on the grounds of cost. Today this manoeuvre would not be allowed by the Traffic Commissioners, not just because of Highway Code regulations but, with today's volume of traffic, it would be just too dangerous! The young girl, walking past the bungalows in Coppice Road, glances over her shoulder at the sound of the reversing trolleybus. *J. C. Brown*

Above On 10 August 1960 Sunbeam W4 trolleybus 454 (EJW 454) waits at the picking-up stop at the Finchfield Road West terminus. Unlike most modern trolleybuses elsewhere in Britain, where the silence of a parked trolleybus would be occasionally broken by the hum of the compressor building up air in the brake tanks, in Wolverhampton this did not happen as the trolleys had vacuum brakes. This trolleybus had re-entered service only four months earlier with its new Charles Roe body, and is still sporting green-painted wings, which will be repainted black at the vehicle's first repaint in January 1963. It has completed the reversing procedure in Coppice Road and is waiting outside the row of old cottages on the right. Behind the 'BUS UNLOADING ONLY' stop in the foreground is a row of bay-windowed late-Victorian terraces that look strangely out of place, perhaps better suiting an area much nearer the town centre. The New Inn disappeared in the 1970s and was replaced by a floral traffic island – ah, such is progress! *J. C. Brown*

Below The 43 motorbus service travelled past the New Inn and along Castlecroft Road before turning into Windmill Lane and reaching its terminus at Castlecroft Avenue, just short of the Staffordshire County boundary. The post-war concrete bus shelter is typical of those found in suburbia, and this one is standing opposite the Castlecroft Hotel where 118 (7118 UK) waits to return to Wolverhampton in about 1965. The bus is a Guy 'Arab' V with a Weymann H41/31F body, which had entered service in November 1963 as part of the trolleybus replacement fleet of diesel-engined buses. Unusually it was fitted not with a Gardner 6LW unit but an AEC AV590 9.6-litre engine. This was an option offered by Guy Motors for its 'Arab' V model in the 1960s, but these ten buses for the company's home town, of which 118 was the eighth, appear to have been unique. The bus survived into WMPTE ownership and was not withdrawn until 1974. *D. R. Harvey collection*

Jeffcock Road

The trolleybus service to Jeffcock Road was re-routed on 8 November 1937, having previously been part of the Bradmore via Great Brickkiln Street service. The latter had opened on 10 April 1933 as the 12 route beginning in the town centre in Victoria Square. When the trolleybus route alterations to Finchfield and Merry Hill were established, the Bradmore link, passing the General Cemetery at the northern end of Jeffcock Road, was abandoned. On 13 May 1946 the town terminus was altered from Stafford Street to Whitmore Street in order to relieve the congestion of waiting south-west-bound trolleybuses, and at the same time the Jeffcock Road service was re-numbered 9 and became part of the cross-town route to Amos Lane, near Wednesfield, which had formerly been the northern half of the 12A service to Finchfield.

Throughout the war years the route seemed to attract the oldest trolleybuses in the fleet; in particular the increasingly decrepit six-wheelers from the 1931 to 1933 batches were regularly used until their sagging bodies creaked and groaned over the cobbles for the last time in about 1947. The cross-town service continued until 29 September 1963, when the Jeffcock Road half of the route was closed, leaving the northern Amos Lane end, which had been the original 9 route, to continue until 3 November 1963. The nearby south-western trolleybus routes to Finchfield and Merry Hill also closed on this latter date.

The Jeffcock Road route itself was in many ways very similar to the Nechells trolleybus route in Birmingham, serving an old-established industrial area and its outward half being lined by late-19th-century housing. On arrival in the town centre from Amos Lane, the route started outside the Territorial Army Headquarters in Stafford Street opposite the Wolverhampton & Staffordshire Technical College. This was built on the site of the Stuart-built Old Deanery and opened in 1933; since 1992 it has been part of the University of Wolverhampton. After the terminus alteration of 1946, the trolleybuses negotiated a new one-way loop around Westbury Street and into Broad Street, where they joined the Penn (11) route. Climbing up to Princes Square and bearing right into Lichfield Street, the trolleybuses passed the elegant Victorian buildings of this part of the town centre before reaching Queen Square beneath the shadows of St Peter's Church.

Turning into Victoria Street at the Edwardian-built Queen's Arcade, the service descended to Worcester Street where, in medieval times, Wolverhampton's only central watercourse, Puddle Brook, once flowed. At the White Hart public house the route turned right, and quite suddenly the central shopping district was left behind as the trolleybuses entered Great Brickkiln Street and an area of old-established heavy industry. Factories such as the Elgin Tin Plate Works, the Raglan Spring factory, the Reliance Hemp and Rope Works and the Cleveland Rope and Twine Company were interspersed with tiny terraced houses and courtyards, while one of the town's first Board Schools was also located in Great Brickkiln Street. On reaching the junction with Oak Street, the trolleybuses turned southwards and ran along Owen Road through rows of late-Victorian terraced housing. This part of the route has remained little altered since the trolleybuses were abandoned, unlike the section along Great Brickkiln Street which is but a pale shadow of its former important self.

Having arrived at St Chad's Church in Owen Road, the 9 route turned right and went up the steep climb in Rayleigh Road, then passed through the last of the area's terraced housing built before the First World War. At the T-junction at Jeffcock Road, the passengers, officially at least, were dropped off and the trolleybuses turned right for about 100 yards, following the line of the old Bradmore route. They then reversed into Downham Place, a 1920s-developed side road, and pulled back across Jeffcock Road to pick up outside a row of shops. In the late 1950s, to avoid traffic hold-ups, this terminus was abandoned and moved back into Rayleigh Road.

Below Parked in Whitmore Street is 8-feet-wide Sunbeam F4 trolleybus 466 (FJW 466). This terminus was introduced on 13 May 1946 and allowed the 9 service to wait in an uncongested side street before moving off to Jeffcock Road. The trolleybus is lying over before heading back to Jeffcock Road on the 9 service on 20 September 1961. In the background, in Stafford Street, is the Wolverhampton & Staffordshire Technical College, whose first stage, the Engineering Block, was opened by Princess Mary. Also parked in Whitmore Street on the wrong side of the road is a wartime Guy 'Arab' II, rebodied by Charles Roe. Mr Gorse's newsagent and tobacconist shop is a microcosm of life in the 1960s. On the wall are chewing-gum machines for Beech-Nut and Wrigley brands, and while Player's cigarettes are still with us, who can forget Capstan – for full strength (*cough!*). This was in pre-tabloid days when the *Daily Express* and the *News of the World* were about as salacious as papers could get. It was left to the weekly magazine *Reveille*, with its news-stand headline 'Requiem for a Schoolgirl', to provide the juicier stories. *J. C. Brown*

Bottom A pair of Austin A35 vans are parked outside the Perfection Fireplaces showrooms in Broad Street as trolleybus 463 (FJW 463), a Sunbeam F4 with a Park Royal body of 1948, turns out of Westbury Street on Thursday 21 September 1961. Until only a few years earlier Westbury Street had contained old courtyards dating from the late 18th century, representing some of the worst housing in the town, with single standpipes supplying water for all the households around the dilapidated courts. The trolleybus overhead for the single right turn out of Westbury Street joins the loop of the wiring for the Penn and Wednesfield trolleybus routes that ascend Broad Street. In the background, alongside the Birmingham Canal, is the British Waterways Broad Street warehouse, formerly known as the Shropshire Union Wharf. The cast-iron parapet railings of the bridge over the canal that led into Wednesfield Road are visible above the approaching AEC Monarch Mk III two-axle lorry. Halfway down Broad Street on the right-hand side is Fryer Street, which in the 1750s marked the eastern boundary of the town. In later years it led through to Victoria Square and contained the famous 1899 premises of Chubb, the lockmaker, and the synagogue in central Wolverhampton. *J. C. Brown*

Right   As was usual after the abandonment of a trolleybus system, the electrical infrastructure was removed with almost indecent haste. By 1968 virtually everything had gone in the town centre, although the traction pole at the centre of Princes Square, on which traffic lights, street lights, instruction signs and I dare say the town's Christmas lights were suspended, was deemed too useful to remove. Barking its way across the wide square in front of the old Criterion Hotel, from the Grand Theatre end of Lichfield Street, is Guy 'Arab' IV motorbus 1 (SUK 1), fitted with a rear-entrance Metro-Cammell body. This bus entered service in March 1957 and had a locally manufactured Meadows 6DC engine. It is working on the 9 service to Jeffcock Road, which had been converted from trolleybus operation,

after 27 years, on 29 September 1963. On the right, displaying its sliding forward-entrance door, is Guy 'Arab' V 170 (GJW 170C), which had entered service in July 1965. *D. R. Harvey collection*

Below   Travelling along Lichfield Street from Princes Square is rebodied Sunbeam W4 trolleybus 434 (EJW 434). It is about to pass The Posada public house, owned by Birmingham-based Ansells Brewery, which is well 'buried' in the splendid row of late-Victorian properties that stand opposite the Art Gallery. The trolleybus is about to go from the two-track section of overhead at the Princes Square end

into the four-track section that began outside the District Bank. This was a notorious dewirement spot in the town centre's trolleybus wiring, and the disappearing 619 (FJW 619), a Sunbeam F4 with the usual Park Royal H28/26R body, working towards Princes Square, has just approached this spot where the four wires funnel into two. Glimpsed between the two trolleybuses is one of the two Harper Brothers former Metalcraft coach-bodied Leyland 'Royal Tiger' PSU1/12s of 1951, which had been fitted in 1961 with Harper-finished Metal Section DP44F bodies that were very similar to those fitted by Midland Red to its S14 single-deckers. *J. C. Brown*

Below The Jeffcock Road trolleybus service turned from Lichfield Street and Queen Square into Victoria Street, leaving behind at the top of the hill the ugly 1960s five-storey block that belonged to Times Furnishing, and which had so cruelly replaced the lovely old Hippodrome Theatre. On 29 April 1962 trolleybus 446 (EJW 446), one of the early post-war Sunbeam W4s rebodied by Roe with attractive-looking 60-seater bodies, in this case re-entering service on 19 January 1962, is passing the early Regency Star & Garter hotel and public house with its much later mock-Tudor frontage. All the buildings on the right, including the Queen's Arcade on the corner of Queen Square, and Chas Hunter's unfortunately named Rubber House, were later demolished to make way for the Mander Shopping Centre. Parked outside Beattie's Department Store on the left is a 1954 Birmingham-registered Humber Hawk Mark VI saloon, while turning out of Queen Square is a Ford Consul EOTA four-door saloon, which is carrying learner plates. *J. C. Brown*

Opposite above A noticeable feature of Victoria Street was this inter-war block of shops, which appears as though it has been transported from a Hollywood film lot, looking, as it still does today, simply out of place – attractive enough, but just in the wrong place. These retail premises, which also had frontages on Salop Street, were opened in 1927, having been built by a Birmingham-based estate company, replacing earlier, time-expired buildings. Among them is Aldridge's Restaurant, which had been established in the older premises in 1886, and two branches of County Wallpapers. On the corner of Skinner Street and Victoria Street, off to the right, was an almost town-centre-sized Boots the Chemist. This site would have overlooked the experimental Wolseley-bus-operated Penn Fields service of 1905, which used Skinner Street as its terminus until it was replaced by the more reliable Penn Fields tram service in September 1909. The older buildings in Worcester Street, beyond the junction with Salop Street, date from the late 19th century. Marshall's

furniture store is located in one of the blocks of quite large three-storey shops of a type found around the edges of town centres all over the country. This late-Victorian urban growth spread out along the main radial routes from town centres and eventually linked up with outlying former hamlets such as Penn, so forming a continuous line of urban development. It is near this point in Victoria Street that Wolverhampton's 'silent service' crosses the long-since-culverted Pudding Brook. Unloading its passengers on 20 September 1961, having travelled into town from Jeffcock Road, is trolleybus 414 (DUK 14), a 1945 Sunbeam W4 chassis that had originally been fitted with a 'utility' body, but was rebodied with a replacement Park Royal body in March 1952. A most unusual car is the pre-war Daimler Six, which is crossing the Salop Street junction. The trolleybus is being overtaken by a Ford Thames 300E 5cwt van, while the car pulling out in front of the Austin Minivan is a mid-1960 Ford Consul 204E. *J. C. Brown*

Below right On 1 September 1961, waiting for the 17-year-old Midland Counties Dairy Electricar battery milk float to turn right out of Great Brickkiln Street into Worcester Street, is Park Royal-rebodied Sunbeam W4 416 (DUK 16). It is only four months after the Penn routes and the Jeffcock Road services had been re-instated on 2 May following the completion of the pedestrian subways beneath the Salop Street-School Street junction, and 416 is working out of town on the 9 route. On the near corner of Great Brickkiln Street, beyond the row of mid-Victorian shops that includes Quality Cleaners, is the White Hart public house, built in 1923 in a heavily mullion-windowed style. The tall three-storey block on the far corner dates from 1909, the shop on the corner being a highly renowned photographic studio owned by a family called Banerjee. The trolleybus wires in the foreground serve the Penn, Penn Fields and Coalway Road routes. Most of the buildings on the left have survived until the present day, while at the time of writing those on the right await refurbishment. *J. C. Brown*

Left Travelling out of town along Great Brickkiln Street is Roe-rebodied Sunbeam W4 trolleybus 422 (DUK 822). It is passing the junction with Salisbury Street, flanked, as nearly all these side roads were, by two corner shops, in this case a fish and chip shop and a butcher. In the intervening years all these late-19th-century premises have been demolished. Just visible above the distant terraces behind the trolleybus is what might have been the replacement for all such properties; this is the top of Grange Court, which with Wulfruna Court, also in Dale Street, were Wolverhampton's first multi-storey flats, dating from about 1960. The long three-storey building in the distance nearer the town centre is the large 19th-century carpet-cleaning factory of Baynell's, which advertised itself as having the 'biggest mangle in Europe'. One long-lost feature of these early 1960s photographs are the Staffordshire blue-brick pavements, which were going out of fashion at the time and were being replaced by concrete slabs. Opposite the trolleybus is Brickkiln Street School, opened in 1878 as one of the original Wolverhampton Board Schools built in response to the 1870 Forster Elementary Education Act. Originally built with a strangely proportioned tower, it survives today as the local area's primary school. It stands next to Lord Street, which contained the Cleveland Rope and Twine Works, one of two rope and hemp factories off Great Brickkiln Street, Reliance Mills being in nearby Shepherd Street. Opposite the school, behind the trolleybus, is Zoar Street, which had a very strong link with road transport in that it was, for many years, the home of Maley & Taunton, the tram component manufacturer. On the corner was the 1920s Royal Oak, which is now the worshipping place of the Seventh Day Adventists. *J. C. Brown*

Below left Turning into the curved western section of Great Brickkiln Street on 29 September 1961 is trolleybus 404 (DJW 904), approaching the junction with Owen Road, where it will turn hard left on its way to Jeffcock Road. The trolleybus is a rebodied Sunbeam W4, which entered service on 1 December 1944 with a Park Royal 'utility' body and was fitted with this Park Royal body during March 1952.

Behind the double-decker to the right are the corrugated-iron premises of Great Brickkiln Street Garage, which with its signs for Goodyear Tyres, Lucas/CAV electrical components and Champion Spark Plugs is a car repair shop rather than a petrol station. The multi-chimneyed houses beyond the garage are on either side of Kimberley Street; they date from the 1890s and survive today. To the immediate left of the trolleybus is the yard of George Shelley's road haulage company, in which is an unidentified second-hand, pre-war, full-fronted coach, with what appears to be a Duple body. On the left is Ash Street, which has since largely disappeared under a housing redevelopment scheme. *J. C. Brown*

Below The shop next to the island at the western end of Great Brickkiln Street is the sort of corner shop that was found in the inner areas of most English towns and cities, and would do justice to Ronnie Barker's BBC television series *Open All Hours*, selling everything imaginable, from Wills's Capstan cigarettes to Colman's Mustard, Lyons and Typhoo Tea, Robin Starch and the relatively 'new-fangled' Birds Eye frozen foods, just some of the signs covering the frontage of the shop. Parked in front of the shop is one of the original Ford Escorts. In production from 1956 to 1960, this was Ford's first factory-built small station wagon; with its 1172cc side-valve engine, it was based on the contemporary Anglia 100E two-door saloon car. Turning out of Great Brickkiln Street into Owen Road is 457 (FJW 457), the second of Wolverhampton's 99 8-feet-wide trolleybuses. This Park Royal-bodied Sunbeam F4 entered service on 3 September 1948, but by this time, 1 September 1961, it had already had its last repaint some six months earlier and had only another four years service in front of it. To the extreme left is Oak Street, with more rows of late-Victorian terraced houses. In 2000, 40 years later, the traffic island in Great Brickkiln Street has gone, as has the shop on the corner. The whole area and most of the housing around the Owen Road junction was renewed in the early 1990s with attractive low-rise houses and maisonettes. Yet the wooden fence on the right has managed to survive! *J. C. Brown*

Below Owen Road linked Great Brickkiln Street with Lea Road, although the trolleybuses only ran for about two-thirds of its length before turning into Rayleigh Road. Just visible to the left of the line of traction poles on the east side of the road is the spire of St Chad's C of E Church. Owen Road is lined by apparently never-ending bay-windowed terraces of tunnel-back houses dating from the last years of the 1890s. It was this style of housing that the 'good burghers' of Victorian Wolverhampton encouraged, rather than the earlier and quite awful back-to-backs, courtyards and tenements that characterised so many other large industrial towns. On Wednesday 20 September 1961, travelling towards the traffic island at Great Brickkiln Street on learner duty is Guy BT 498 (FJW 498), which would in a few months become the last trolleybus to operate on the Penn Fields route. Just visible in the cab alongside the trainee driver is the driving instructor. By coincidence the parked Ford Popular 103G car on the right also carries 'L' plates. This 'sit-up-and-beg' Ford 'Pop' was cheap, cheerful, fairly uncomfortable, slow, thirsty and virtually indestructible, and with its three-speed unsophisticated gearbox was an ideal vehicle in which to be taught to drive. Following the trolleybus is a Commer Superpoise Super Capacity van, overtaking a Wolseley 15/60 saloon that is barely one year old and is parked facing the wrong direction. *J. C. Brown*

Opposite above Having travelled along Owen Road to within 500 yards of Lea Road on the Penn Fields 4 route, the Jeffcock Road trolleybus service reached the junction with Lime Street and Rayleigh Road. On 8 November 1937 the 9 trolleybus had been re-routed via Great Brickkiln Street to serve this part of the town, which had been developed very rapidly during the last decade of the 19th century. The roads were named arboreally, with Ash Street, Elm Street, Oak Street and Lime Street in the vicinity, and reflected a later, more open development of artisan property. The houses belonged to the 'tunnel-back' generation, a product of the terms of the 1875 Public Health Act that effectively put paid to 'back-to-back' housing and the social degradation that it encouraged. The 'tunnel-backs' were well-made and each had its own water supply and outside lavatory. Although they had a narrow street frontage, they extended two or three rooms back from the road and had their own small plot of land behind, which served as their garden. Turning right from Owen Road into Rayleigh Road is Sunbeam W4 trolleybus 416 (DUK 16). On the corner of Owen Road and Lime Street are a couple of shops including Hickman's newsagent and tobacconist and, with the extended sunblind, a grocer and provision merchant. There is also a butcher's shop on the corner of Rayleigh Road, whose heavy-looking sunblind is visible through the lower branches of the large tree behind the Halt sign. Turning left into Owen Road is a Wolverhampton-registered Ford Anglia 105E with 'two-tone' paintwork. *J. C. Brown*

Below right The steepness of the climb out of the Graisley Brook valley up Rayleigh Road from the Owen Road junction to the top at Norfolk Road can be judged from this view of 498 (FJW 498) powering its way up the hill. Behind the trolleybus, at the bottom of the hill opposite the parked pre-war Morris Eight two-door saloon, is the grit bin seen in the previous photograph. The houses on the hill are slightly newer than those in Owen Road, having tiny walled front gardens, many of which are bounded by privet hedges. Beyond Norfolk Road, Rayleigh Road descended gently until the junction with Jeffcock Road was reached. The Park Royal-bodied trolleybus is being used on learner duty. Wolverhampton Corporation adopted the policy of teaching its newly recruited trainee drivers on a trolleybus that was driven between normal service vehicles, unlike certain operators who employed learner drivers on normal passenger-carrying trolleybuses. That unusual practice was quite legal because trolleys came under the jurisdiction of Railway Regulations rather than Road Traffic Acts, allowing for the tuition of drivers under service conditions. *J. C. Brown*

Below By the time this view was taken, on 16 September 1961, the original 9 route terminus outside the shops on the left had been abandoned, and the trolleybuses deposited their passengers at the end of Rayleigh Road, officially at least, for it was the normal practice to allow passengers to stay aboard until the trolleybus stopped prior to reversing into Downham Place, the road on the right being passed by the Austin 10hp four-door saloon car. Sunbeam F4 trolleybus 465 (FJW 465) is turning right into Jeffcock Road empty – but for one furtive person upstairs! – before travelling the 50 yards or so to a point just beyond Downham Place. The trolleybus overhead has a reversing triangle and, unlike the awful arrangement at the 12 route terminus at Finchfield, the trolleybus reverses into Downham Place before retracing its tracks back to the new terminus in Rayleigh Road. Parked on the forecourt of Wassall's car showroom on the extreme right is a 1946 Coventry-registered Standard 8hp drophead coupé and a comparatively rare 1670cc Standard Ensign – only 18,852 were produced between 1957 and 1961. On the left, parked in front of the shops, are a Ford Thames 300E 5cwt van, a couple of Morris Oxford Series IV, an Austin A40 Farina two-door saloon and a white-painted Austin A30 saloon car. Today's bus service frequency is a far cry from that operated by the trolleybuses, which ran at a frequency of between 12 and 15 minutes, and also ran on Sundays; it takes a solitary bus to operate the present-day TWM service, which is partially interspersed by a minibus service that at the time of writing is operated by Zak's of Great Barr. *J. C. Brown*

Opposite below Standing in Downham Place, having reversed from Jeffcock Road, is 8-feet-wide trolleybus 463 (FJW 463), a Park Royal-bodied Sunbeam F4 that entered service on 18 September 1948 and would remain in use until 9 June 1963, when it would become another victim of the Penn and Penn Fields trolleybus route closures. Opposite the trolleybus is the same Ford Thames 5cwt van whose rear was seen in the previous photograph. The trolleybus is about to turn right into Jeffcock Road and pass the original terminus located just beyond Glover's Stores at the end of the block of shops. On the right is the Wassall Motor Company, on whose forecourt is HNP 500, a Rover six-light P3 series Seventy-Five, which was registered in Worcestershire in April 1949. The lady walking past the racks of greengroceries on the right is about to pass another one of Wassall's bargains, a Citroën Light Fifteen, better known as the 'Traction' model. This larger though similar-looking six-cylinder car with an extended boot is the vehicle made famous by the BBC television series *Maigret*, starring Rupert Davies as Georges Simenon's cerebral Parisian Inspector of Detectives. The Light Fifteen was not an import from France, as between 1935 and 1955, with a break for the war, it was manufactured in the UK at Slough, Middlesex. The greengrocer was owned for many years by the Brooks family, who had Stall No 1 in Wolverhampton's central Market Place. Originally Wassall's premises had also been owned for many years by a family grocer called Jubb. Legend has it that for some obscure reason a gypsy curse was put on the premises, and after the Jubbs retired the shop changed hands with alarming rapidity. No one did well there, and even the car showroom only lasted a few years, closing down in 1962. However, by about 1978 the curse must have begun to wear off, as a grocer remained in the shop for about 20 years, only leaving quite recently. *J. C. Brown*

This page Turning from Downham Place into Jeffcock Road on 10 February 1962 is Park Royal-rebodied Sunbeam W4 trolleybus 407 (DJW 907). Beyond the trolleybus on the right-hand side of Jeffcock Road is the long-established General Cemetery, though in recent years it has been known simply as Jeffcock Road Cemetery. This interdenominational facility covering some 24 acres opened in 1850, having cost the then enormous sum of £12,000 to set up. Even as late as 1902 it was still at the western boundary of the town facing across open land to the old Merridale House, better known today as Bantock House. The trolleybus will pass the Austin A35 car on the right, then turn left into

Rayleigh Road to pick up passengers before going across town to Amos Lane at The Pheasant at Wood End Road.

Although the seasons are different and those trees in Jeffcock Road that have survived the intervening 38 years are in full leaf, the view along Jeffcock Road towards the distant cemetery and the junction with Merridale Road at Bantock Park has hardly changed at all. The row of shops on the right, including the Jeffcock Road Stores and the Jeffcock Chippy, survive, and the house on the far corner of Downham Place still has its fine, neatly cut hedge, which in trolleybus days was the source of some acrimony as the Corporation said it obstructed the view around the corner as the trolleybuses reversed. This was true if the conductor stayed on the back platform as many were wont to do, instead of standing behind the reversing vehicle in order to assist the driver. Anyway, the hedge survived and, unlike the long-since-gone trolleybuses, thrives in the same owner's tender care. *J. C. Brown/D. R. Harvey*

Below The original Jeffcock Road terminus was, not altogether surprisingly, actually in Jeffcock Road. After it was moved round the corner into Rayleigh Road in the late 1950s, the outbound destination blind display was unhelpfully left unaltered, reading 'JEFFCOCK ROAD VIA GREAT BRICKKILN STREET'. Parked outside the tobacconist in Jeffcock Road, with its signs for Turf, Woodbine and Player's cigarettes, is trolleybus 432 (DUK 832). It is 21 July 1951 and the vehicle is a five-year-old Sunbeam W4. Although it entered service in June 1946, at a time when Park Royal was beginning to deliver bodies to peace-time specification, this trolleybus arrived with what was termed a 'relaxed' utility body. In reality, all this meant was that it had a total of ten opening windows instead of the previously allowed four, and upholstered seating. Strangely, this wartime body-style, first produced on a trolleybus for Reading Corporation in April 1943, remained in production until as late as December 1946, when two vehicles were delivered to Pontypridd UDC. Trolleybus 432 is parked alongside the very 1930s-looking cantilever-styled concrete bus shelter, while behind it is another icon of that decade, the concrete GPO telephone box. In June 1957 the Corporation decided that 16 new bodies were required for its trolleybus fleet in order to give it some sort of parity with the motorbus fleet. Trolleybuses 418-433 all re-entered service with their new Roe H32/28R bodies between August 1958 and October 1959, 432 being the last to appear in its new guise. *J. Hughes*

Below left When the 'new' terminus of the Jeffcock Road 9 trolleybus route was established in Rayleigh Road during the last half of the 1950s, intending passengers lost their shelter, but gained a bench, which enabled them to sit down and get wet! Although less convenient than the original terminus, Rayleigh Road was quieter and was therefore a safer haven for vehicles awaiting their allocated departure time back into town. On 21 May 1961 438 (EJW 438), with its by now one-year-old body, its windscreen surrounds still unsullied with 'a lick of paint', waits to load up in Rayleigh Road, its destination blind having been turned round to read 'AMOS LANE VIA FALLINGS PARK'. In the background are the large terraced villas in Jeffcock Road, while emerging from the Lea Road direction is a black Austin A40 Somerset car. The Jeffcock Road end of the cross-town 9 trolleybus route was abandoned on 29 September 1963, so by the end of that year all the trolleybus routes to the south and west of the town had succumbed to the motorbus. The northern half of the 9 route did not last much longer, being withdrawn on 3 November 1963, when no fewer than seven trolleybus routes were abandoned. *J. C. Brown*

Tettenhall

The Tettenhall tram and trolleybus routes and the bus services that used Tettenhall Road to reach places beyond the boundary were undoubtedly part of Wolverhampton's 'Premier Line'. All these modes of public transport passed through some of the most exquisite housing built in the town during the Regency and Victorian periods along a road attractively lined with mature lime, plane and elm trees. Although not the longest route served by the Corporation, Tettenhall Road is one of the oldest roads in the town, but was rebuilt as a wide, sweeping Thomas Telford-designed road through Newbridge and across the Smestow Valley before reaching Tettenhall UDC. Tettenhall has somehow managed to retain the feel of a village, even though it was so close to the Wolverhampton boundary.

The Wolverhampton Tramways Company opened its horse-tram service from Queen Square on 1 May 1878 and this survived until after the take-over of the company's tram lines on 1 May 1900. As part of the requirement for an electric tram route to serve the West Park Exhibition, the most important event of national and regional interest to occur in Wolverhampton for many years, the new Lorain system trams began to run to New Hampton Road West on 1 May 1901. An extension link was built to join this route with the Newbridge horse-tram replacement service, opened for the new electric tramcars from Victoria Square via Chapel Ash on 12 June 1902. This was extended to the Dog & Gun in Upper Green, Wergs Road, Tettenhall, on 13 September 1902.

The electric tram service continued unaltered on the Lorain Surface Contact system until 5 October 1921, when it became the penultimate tram route to be converted to the more normal overhead method of current collection. The conversion of the Tettenhall tram route to trolleybus operation occurred on 29 November 1927, and from that time until its closure on 30 June 1963 the No 1 trolleybus ran a service with a frequency of between 5 and 8 minutes. It seemed to be the preserve of the larger-seating six-wheeled trolleybuses until well into the dark days of the Second World War, then from 1948 onwards it was usually operated by the then new 8-feet-wide Guy BTs or Sunbeam F4s.

After the closure of the trolleybus service, the latest Guy 'Arab' IV and V double-deckers operated the service until June 1967, when a new generation of what ultimately proved to be unsuccessful Daimler 'Roadliner' and AEC 'Swift' single-deckers were tried out for about six weeks, before the route reverted, much to the relief of crew and passengers alike, to double-deck operation.

The Tettenhall route was an extremely straightforward one. In electric tram days it started in Victoria Square and passed along Lichfield Street into Queen Square. Here it followed the old horse-tram route before descending Darlington Street, passing at No 45 the former horse-tram depot and offices of the Wolverhampton Tramways Company and entering Chapel Ash. The Chapel Ash area, together with the town end of Tettenhall Road, was laid out in the 20 years after the Napoleonic Wars as the first suburb of the town, and the whole area was graced with elegantly designed houses, the best of which survive today.

Passing the Halfway House public house at Paget Road, Tettenhall Road, which was already a wide tree-lined thoroughfare, widened even more as it passed the Wolverhampton Girls' High School at St Jude's Road, before slowly descending into the Smestow Brook valley at Newbridge. Here it passed the other horse-tram depot just east of the junction with New Hampton Road West, nearly opposite the premises of the present-day commercial Beacon Radio station. Crossing Smestow Brook, the Staffordshire & Worcestershire Canal of 1772 and the GWR's Wombourne railway line, the route negotiated the 1 in 22 climb out of the valley through a cutting known as The Rock, made by Thomas Telford, before emerging into the flat, wide-open spaces of Upper Green,

Tettenhall. Eventually, in bus days, after the formation of the WMPTE, the Tettenhall service was extended into the village area.

Beyond the terminus of the 1 trolleybus route, along Wergs Road, Corporation-operated country buses served the villages and towns straddling the main A41. These services had been acquired mainly from the Midland Red on 2 March 1927, and the extension of the town's boundaries under the terms of the Wolverhampton Corporation Act of 1926 also gave the Transport Department unrestricted

access to areas beyond the trolleybus termini. Services to Wergs, Burnhill Green and Beckbury (27), Albrighton, Cosford, Tong and Norton (49) and Donington (89) went deep into the Staffordshire countryside. These routes were usually operated by a variety of pre-war and post-war single-deckers, although as demand grew less specialised double-deckers were employed. In later years these routes used the new bus station adjacent to Railway Drive, opened on 9 May 1961 and ever afterwards referred to as the 'country bus station'.

Below Although land had been acquired for a small bus station between Railway Street and Railway Drive as long ago as 1953, the facility was not sanctioned until the end of that decade, and a small bus station was opened on 9 May 1960, replacing the somewhat ad hoc parking arrangements in the Horseley Fields and St James's Square area. The Railway Drive loading area for Midland Red buses in front of the High Level Railway Station also moved into this site, leaving only the 17 route to Bridgnorth to soldier on from its terminus on the forecourt of the old GWR Low Level Station. The 49 service to Albrighton and Tong had originally been numbered 29, but on 13 June 1949 it was renumbered in order to allow the trolleybus service jointly worked with Walsall Corporation Motors to keep that municipality's 29 route number. The Tong service had been initiated by Midland Red on 1 March 1922 as part of the 'Wolverhampton Area Agreement', and by 1928 it was being

operated by the Corporation. Seen here in March 1961, not long before its first withdrawal, 383 (DUK 383), the second of just two wartime 'relaxed' utility Park Royal-bodied Daimlers allocated to Wolverhampton, both being fitted with the less common Daimler CD6 8.6-litre engine, waits at the bus station before heading out through Tettenhall to Tong. The 'shortworking' service of the 49 route was the 51, which went, again via Chapel Ash and Tettenhall Road, to terminate at Wergs Post Office, and the second bus is working on this route. It is a 1950 Daimler CVG6 with a Brush H29/25R body, one of the early post-war vehicles that became the real workhorses of the motorbus fleet. *C. Aston*

Opposite above Leaving the Railway Drive bus station is 122 (122 DDA), the first of 25 Park Royal-bodied Guy 'Arab' Vs that entered service in the week before Christmas 1963. They were purchased as direct trolleybus replacement

vehicles and could be distinguished by their very broad windscreens. Unlike the Strachan-bodied buses that succeeded them, the Park Royal bodies, although looking similar to the contemporary Metro-Cammell 'Orion' lightweight bodies, were quite long-lived. This vehicle, for example, had an 11-year life, which was probably curtailed by the WMPTE policy of ridding itself, albeit prematurely, of all front-engined double-deckers. The bus is working on the 39 service to Albrighton, and is crossing Victoria Square before turning into Lichfield Street and reaching Princes Square. It has the usual electrically operated doors, the control mechanism for which is contained behind what looks like a blank destination box just behind the sliding door. *M. Fenton*

Below One of the unsuccessful AEC 'Swift' MP2Rs, 710 (NJW 710E), crosses Victoria Square in June 1967 when brand new. It is operating on the former trolleybus 1 route to Tettenhall, but will be replaced within a few weeks, as One Man Operation was quickly considered unsuitable for this normally heavily loaded arterial route. Unfortunately the buses themselves were not a success. Neither the 'Swifts' nor the 'Roadliners' gave the mechanical reliability that might have been expected from their respective long-established manufacturers. The Strachan B54D bodies, which looked very similar to the ill-fated London Transport MB class, were also not particularly good and their panels quickly began to 'crinkle', indicating that all was not well beneath the surface. In common with the Strachan-bodied Guy 'Arab' Vs, these single-deckers were destined to have short lives, an unfortunate result of 'buying cheaply' – this bus only lasted in service for six years. Although displaying a 'Pay As You Enter' sign, the single-decker has on board a conductress, who will not only take the fares but also assist passengers with the unfamiliar centre exit arrangement of these buses. On the left is the Sir Tatton Sykes public house, while parked in Victoria Square are the black and white Austin A60 private hire taxis, whose paint scheme might have been more at home in Athens than Wolverhampton. *M. Fenton*

Left Leaving Victoria Square, the Tettenhall trolleybuses passed along Lichfield Street, passing the Victoria Hotel on the corner of the Square, and the canopied Grand Theatre. The latter dated from December 1894 and towers above the two parked Jaguar cars, the first of which is a 3.4-litre Mark I model, while the lighter-coloured one is a later wide-tracked Mark II. They are parked alongside the porticoed entrance of the General Post Office, which is flanked by two sentry-box-like telephone boxes. Wartime Sunbeam W4 trolleybus 410 (DJW 940), rebodied by Park Royal and re-entering service on 25 April 1952, positively sparkles in the low evening sunshine of Thursday 14 June 1962. It had only come back into service a few days earlier after receiving a full overhaul and repaint, which would prove to be its last. Although officially withdrawn on 31 July 1965, since 31 October 1964 it had only seen service as a driver training vehicle. On the extreme left is one of the 40-69 batch of reverse JW-registered Guy 'Arab' IVs with a forward-entrance MCW body dating from 1960. *J. C. Brown*

Below left The 1A motorbus service to Wergs largely covered the Tettenhall trolleybus route, although it had its town terminus in Queen Street. With its Georgian terraces Queen Street was one of the town's most prestigious streets, but after the 1880s development of Lichfield Street and the re-alignment of Railway Drive it was largely passed by in the late 19th century redevelopment of the town centre, which explains the survival of so much of the original property. Waiting in Queen Street during the late 1940s are three of the Corporation's 'Arab' models. The leading bus on the Wergs service is 361 (DJW 561), one of just two Park Royal-bodied 'Arab' Mark I 5LWs that entered service in March 1943.

They could easily be distinguished from the later Mark II 'Arabs' by their short Leyland-style front wings, rather than the curly-ended ones of the similarly bodied 362 (DJW 762), which was delivered in September of the same year. Further down Queen Street is an unidentified Weymann-bodied Guy 'Arab' II from the 377-381 batch, all of which had entered service in early 1946; it still sports its wartime grey livery. Unlike the two older buses in front of it, it has the standard Wolverhampton front destination boxes. Only the 'Arab' IIs would be rebodied by Roe in 1952. *B. Baker collection*

Below Leaving Princes Square on its way out of town and passing the Art Gallery in Lichfield Street is an unidentified direct-staircase tramcar, still fitted with an open top and dating from the 1904-05 period. As early as 1911 the position of tram drivers, standing in the open vestibule, was coming into question; although they were given greatcoats and waterproofs, they were exposed to the elements, and as a result the health of the motormen was becoming an issue. This was not necessarily through any philanthropic concern, but purely on the grounds of economy, as the drivers' absenteeism due to illness was becoming a severe problem. As a result, between 1911 and 1917 all the trams were fitted with vestibuled platforms. As the Tettenhall route was converted from the Lorain Surface Contact system on 5 October 1921, this picture must date from the years immediately after the end of the First World War. The 1890s row of shops on the corner of Lichfield Street and Princes Square would have graced any town or city in the land; the corner site is occupied by Bradley's Toy & Fancy Goods Emporium, while alongside the tram is Christie's tailors, a confectioner's shop and a pub. *J. Hughes collection*

Below On a sunny day in August 1929 two Wolverhampton Corporation buses stand at the junction of Lichfield Street and Princes Square waiting for the recently installed traffic lights to change in their favour. The leading vehicle is trolleybus 55 (UK 5955), working towards the Victoria Square terminus of the Tettenhall route. It is a one-year-old Guy BTX six-wheeler and is fitted with a Christopher Dodson 61-seater body. Despite sporting enclosed staircases, top covers, fully glazed cabs and a level of comfort and performance that could never have been achieved by the trams they replaced, by about 1933 trolleybus body design development would make these five-year-old vehicles look very antiquated. Just visible is the bamboo trolley retrieving pole carried alongside the offside rear bogie. Behind the bus is a rather basic-looking four-door touring car typical of those produced in the mid-1920s, and behind that is normal-control motorbus 49 (DA 9049), also bodied by Dodson with a 55-seat capacity. It was Wolverhampton's only Guy BKX model, as it had a Daimler-Knight sleeve-valve engine, a six-cylinder CV35 unit of 5.76-litre capacity; producing about 85bhp at 2,400rpm but burning engine oil at a prodigious rate. It was also only the third top-covered six-wheeler in the motorbus

fleet and only the second to have an enclosed staircase. It is working on the 12 route from Finchfield and is passing Lichfield Passage; the Midland Bank, the pillared building on the left, is the former Metropolitan Bank, which was destined to be occupied by the Midland until 1996. *D. R. Harvey collection*

Opposite bottom It is a sobering thought that the old, bonneted lady sitting on one of the benches in front of the iron railings in Lichfield Street was probably born when 'Prinnie', King George IV, was the monarch! Behind her, sitting on the wall of the Horsman Fountain, is a young girl wearing the then fashionable Edwardian smock-style dress. The Horsman fountain and gardens stand between St Peter's Collegiate Church and Lichfield Street, while beyond them is the impressive yet strangely proportioned Art Gallery, opened on 21 July 1885, with its upper-storey Greco-Roman friezes. Further along Lichfield Street is the Metropolitan Bank. Inbound open-topped tramcar 22, one of the six ER&TCW cars built with reverse staircases and mounted on DuPont trucks, entering service between August and October 1902, stands outside the bank, carrying the ubiquitous destination display 'RAILY STATION'. The row of late-Victorian three-storey and four-storey retail premises has survived into the present day and includes The Posada public house. The buildings represent a period of rapid town centre redevelopment that epitomised the economic confidence of the day and transformed the townscape from what were essentially market areas into important retail centres. The street lighting represents the first type used to illuminate the town centre; they are DC-powered carbon arc lamps, and were replaced before the First World War with the more efficient incandescent type. *J. Hughes collection*

Below With the rebuilt 14th-century tower of the Collegiate Church of St Peter dominating the immediately pre-First World War skyline, the view over Queen Square is one of great animation. Behind the 1866 statue of Prince Albert is the impressive Barclays Bank building designed by Thomas Henry Fleeming in 1876, which replaced the two-storey multi-gabled 18th-century building that occupied the corner site in Lich Gates. Parked on the opposite corner of Lich Gates is a horse-bus belonging to Thomas Bakewell, who was operating on the Compton route between 1912 and 1913. In this transition period of transport, an open touring car speeds past the horse-bus into Lichfield Street, while parked alongside the Prince Albert statue is that quintessential symbol of late-Victorian life, the hansom cab. Two of the three electric tramcars are open-topped, although interestingly both are vestibuled, while the top-covered tram, 49, still has open vestibules; the one passing Lich Gates is travelling to Wergs Road, along Tettenhall Road. In the foreground are public lavatories opened in 1902, which included the town's first facility of this type for women. Parked in front of the cabbies' impressive-looking hut is a horse-drawn fire brigade ladder, while on the extreme right is another hansom cab. *J. C. Brown collection*

Below The Tettenhall tram route was the penultimate one to be converted from the Lorain system to the more normal trolleypole and overhead wire method of electric current collection on 5 October 1921. It only ran in this form until 10 July 1927 when the trams stopped running on this, the original tram (albeit horse-tram) route in the town. Car 13, a G. F. Milnes-built tram that entered service in July 1902, has been transformed out of all recognition by the time of this mid-1920s view across Queen Square; although

transformed with vestibules and a top cover, because of Board of Trade Regulations regarding operation on the narrow 3ft 6in gauge, four-wheeled double-decker tramcars such as 13 could not be fitted with enclosed balconies, and as a result no Wolverhampton tram was so equipped. The strange metal cowling at the bottom of the central vestibule window was so shaped in order to clear the horizontal handbrake wheel. Car 13 is travelling inbound across Queen Square towards the Barclays Bank building and

Lichfield Street. It is passing the stub section of track in the open space behind the intrepid motorcyclist and his sidecar combination, which was installed for shortworkings on the Tettenhall, Penn Fields, Bushbury and Whitmore Reans tram services. To the left of the tram is Exchange Street, while the tall building with the three columns is the National Provincial Bank, originally built for the Staffordshire Bank. *Commercial postcard*

Below Looking over Darlington Street from the tower of the Methodist Chapel on the corner of School Street shows the late 1890s landscape of Wolverhampton. In essence, the town was extended beyond its Georgian area during the rapid, early expansion of industry and corresponding housing in the 19th century, but during this period two unusual things occurred.

First, there was, initially at least, very little infilling with new buildings either in the town centre or along the main arterial streets. Second, the new industrial areas were distinct, fairly confined areas beyond the limits of the Georgian town. This can be seen in this view looking towards the distant Chapel Ash area below the imposing presence of St Mark's Church. The Victorian town fathers controlled Wolverhampton's growth with 'artisans' terraces and more expensive villa-type blocks for the better-off, and virtually eliminated the awful back-to-back houses found in other large industrial urban areas such as Birmingham. Darlington Street was completed in 1820 from High Green to Salop Street, through land belonging to Lord Darlington, and connected with the new Wolverhampton turnpike at Chapel Ash; as a result it was lined with lovely pre-Victorian 19th-century buildings. The horse-tram coming up Darlington Street from Tettenhall is being pulled by a third 'trace' horse, which helped the other brace of horses up the hill. The tram is passing Birch Street on the right and is about 50 yards beyond the Wolverhampton Tramway Company's horse-tram depot. On the right, in the middle distance, is the impressively large and still fairly new Park Brewery established in 1890, owned by Wolverhampton & Dudley Breweries, better known as Banks's, who still brew on the site. *J. C. Brown collection*

Below The Darlington Street of the Edwardian era was an impressive thoroughfare lined with the Regency buildings that had appeared when it was first developed. In addition there was a considerable amount of impressive late-Victorian infilling along the street. One such building was the Wesleyan Chapel, from which the previous picture was taken; with its two cupola towers, it was built in 1901 on the

corner of School Street, which is behind the 'ALL CARS STOP HERE' fare stage tram stop on the left. Occupying the other corner is Waterloo House, which contains the premises of Pickens, a firm of clothiers, while next door to it, off the photograph, is Graham & Fortnums Ltd, a high-class gentlemen's tailors. The building on the right, on the Waterloo Road South corner, is the offices of the Wolverhampton Gas Company, which proudly show that it dates from 1880. This building was demolished in 1939 and replaced by a building that, although opened in the second year of the war, presaged 1950s designs and has successfully outlived its apparently more illustrious predecessor. Beyond the tramcar, going all the way down Darlington Street towards Chapel Ash and the distant St Mark's Church with its impressive tower, are the much smaller, original 1830s buildings. The tram working out of town on the Tettenhall route is car 21, one of five ER&TCW open-top, reverse-staircase 48-seaters that were equipped for the Lorain system. Later in life they would become vestibuled and dual-fitted for working on Wolverhampton & District routes that used the normal overhead current collection. The Tettenhall route was converted to overhead current collection on 5 October 1921, but this did not save the system, since as early as March 1923 Wolverhampton Council concurred with the Tramway Committee that the Wednesfield route be converted to trolleybuses. Despite the capital expenditure of replacing the Lorain Surface Contact system, the Tettenhall route was converted to trolleybus operation on 29 November 1927, while the last of the 'native' tram routes to Bilston was abandoned and also converted to trolleybuses on 26 August 1928. At least the cost of the new materials was partially offset by the use of the reasonably new tram infrastructure. *J. Hughes collection*

Below On 9 September 1962, waiting at the School Street traffic lights having come part-way down Darlington Street, is Wolverhampton's very last trolleybus, 654 (FJW 654), which was also the last trolleybus built by Guy Motors, as chassis number BT 37023. Entering service on 8 April 1950, it was withdrawn some 15 years later and donated to the National Trolleybus Association, with whom it still resides, albeit requiring a lot of attention. Post-war Guy trolleybuses were something of a rarity, which was rather a surprise in view of their pre-war popularity, with Belfast Corporation having the only 70 BTX six-wheelers to be built and Wolverhampton the only post-war four-wheelers, of which there were 50. The street scene has hardly altered since the demise of the tramcars some 35 years earlier; a few of the original Regency buildings survive, although the onset of redevelopment can be seen in the distance behind the Austin Big Seven. Following the trolleybus is a whitewall-tyred Jaguar 3.4-litre saloon, registered in Birmingham with a TOL mark in June 1956. These cars, introduced by Sir William Lyons, revolutionised the 'fast saloon' market with their Le Mans-developed pedigree. Capable of 120mph from their 3442cc engines, their Achilles' heel was their narrow rear track, which made them somewhat unstable at speed. It was in one of these cars that the newly crowned World Champion racing driver, Mike Hawthorn, was killed on the Guildford bypass on 22 January 1960. On the corner of School Street is Crawford Wells's bedding shop, offering studio couches as its latest advertised bargain. *J. C. Brown collection*

Below Dominating the Chapel Ash junction is the tall spire of St Mark's Church, consecrated on 19 June 1849 not long after Darlington Street was cut. It remained as a church until 1979, when it was closed as a place of worship; since 1989 it has been used as offices. One of its early vicars was Rev S. Baring Gould, who wrote the words for many fine hymns including 'Onward Christian Soldiers' and 'Through the night of doubt and sorrow'. On this Edwardian day the snow still lies on the road with the tram

tracks tracing their parallel lines from Darlington Street in the foreground towards Chapel Ash. Coming into Wolverhampton from Tettenhall is numerically the Corporation's first double-deck tramcar, number 3. This and cars 6, 9 and the slightly older car 11 were built by G. F. Milnes in 1902 for the opening of the Lorain Surface Contact electric tramcar system to West Park's Industrial & Art Exhibition on 1 May of that year. The trams went along New Hampton Road, while the Tettenhall Road route was opened for traffic a little later on 12 June. Later again, on 13 September, the Tettenhall tram route was extended from Newbridge to the Dog & Gun at Wergs Road, Tettenhall. On the left is the strangely shaped bell-tower of St Mark's School at the junction of Darlington Street and Salop Street, opened in the same year as the church. The horse trough to the left of the tramcar stands at this junction, with St Mark's Road running behind the apse of the church. *J. Hughes collection*

Top right Inching its way past Guy 'Vixen' tower wagon No 7, EUK 770, whose crew are undertaking overhead repairs, is trolleybus 607 (FJW 607). The tower wagon was one of a pair purchased in 1947 with a body by Eagle of Warwick. The Park Royal-bodied Guy BT trolleybus, dating from October 1949, would receive its final repaint within six months and continue in traffic until the abandonment of the Bushbury Hill service on 26 January 1964. It is working on an inbound 1 service from Tettenhall and is turning into Darlington Street, having left Chapel Ash, with St Mark's Church in its tree-lined churchyard on the left. On this spring day, Wednesday 10 May 1961, the daffodils on the triangular traffic island in front of the church are in full bloom. On the right is Littleford's 1950s-built car showroom, advertising the then current Singer Gazelle III convertible. This building looks a little out of place among the three-storey early Victorian buildings next to the crew atop the tower wagon. Parked in front of Littleford's is a Post Office Telephones Morris-Commercial LC-type van painted in the dark green livery and equipped with rubber front wings. Behind the van is a section pillar for the trolleybus DC overhead current supply, while beyond that, with the bicycle propped against it, is the distribution box for the local AC electricity supply for the area. *J. C. Brown*

Above right Travelling into Wolverhampton from Tettenhall on a summer's day in about 1903 is G. F. Milnes-built open-topped tram 9, the noise of its electric motors only interrupted by the clip-clopping of the passing horses and carts. As the policemen on the corner of Chapel Ash and St Mark's Road to the left stand rigidly to attention, the young girl and her mother walk on, oblivious to the photographer. The sheer size of St Mark's Church can be well gauged by the height of its tower emerging from the churchyard trees. On the right are the early-19th-century properties that lined the north side of Chapel Ash, which was developed at the beginning of the Regency period and quickly became the first real suburb of Wolverhampton. It is difficult to believe that this was the case, as today it is almost indistinguishable from the town centre. As a result of its 'suburban' status, it was one of the first areas of the town to receive the 'new-fangled' horse-trams. By 1903, about a year after the introduction of the Lorain Surface Contact electric trams, the measure of their impact can be gauged by the lack of anything else other than horse-drawn traffic. Yet the scene would change again within the decade with the arrival of the motor car, consigning evocative street scenes like this to history. *J. Hughes collection*

Below Galloping through Chapel Ash on its way into the 20th century is one of the former Wolverhampton Tramways Company's horse-trams, travelling towards the town centre. This double-decker was one of the 21-24 class constructed by the Falcon Company, forerunner of the Loughborough-based bodybuilder Brush. The service, as originally operated by the company, opened for traffic on 1 May 1878, charging 2d for the 12-minute service to Newbridge, but on 1 May 1900 the company was taken over by the Corporation. The deal was somewhat protracted, and after a Board of Trade Appeal and an appointed arbiter, the sale went through for £22,500. One of the first tasks of the Corporation was to create a 'corporate image', which initially resulted in the horse-tram drivers being given a full uniform, while the conductors receieved a cap. Corporation operation of the route along Tettenhall Road to Newbridge was only to last until 8 March 1902, when extensive track-laying for the electric trams made it impossible to provide the service. All the horse-tram tracks had to be lifted, as not only were they too light and unbonded, but they were also built to standard 4ft 8½in gauge, while the new electric trams were to run on 3ft 6in gauge tracks, which had been adopted throughout the West Midlands as the norm and allowed for through-running of municipal and company tramcars. In the background is the large Regency house known as Westbourne Place, which occupied the junction of Tettenhall Road, behind the tramcar, and Compton Road. On the right, the suburban shops in Chapel Ash are already becoming well-established. *H. Whitcombe collection*

Below Within the reign of Edward VII, dramatic changes took place in the streets of Britain with the advent, development and improvement of the motor car. Things would never be the same again! This late-Edwardian scene, with the ladies wearing the then fashionable long black skirts and white neck-high blouses, shows that in the few years since the horse-trams went clopping by, most of the three-storey houses on the north side of Chapel Ash have become retail premises. Open-top double-deck tram 30, a G. F. Milnes 51-seater, passes Chapel Ash Post Office on its way towards Darlington

Street. Mounted on Brill 21E trucks, this tram, powered by two BTH GE 60 25hp motors, was destined to remain in this condition until its withdrawal. In the foreground is the well-known horse-trough at the junction of Compton Road and Tettenhall Road, while on the extreme left is Bath Road. On the corner, dominating the junction, is Clark's Carriage & Motor Works. Although there are no cars in sight, there are two early motorcycles parked outside the 'Chapel Ash Motor Cycle Depot' between the disappearing tram and Clark's garage. Clark was already agent for Wolseley-Siddeley cars, the locally manufactured Sunbeam, Minerva – a luxury Belgian marque – Humber and the recently formed Rolls-Royce, established in December 1904. The globe on the roof carries an advertisement for Michelin Tyres, while the garage is already approved by the Automobile Association, which itself had only come into existence in June 1905. The entrance to the garage is in Bath Road, as the corner retail site is occupied by John E. Knight's florist shop, while next door is the Needlecraft Shop. Just to the right of the tram, in the distance, is the gable-end of St Mark's School, while the spire of the church of the same name pierces the skyline on the right above the row of just pre-Victorian houses. *J. Hughes collection*

This page Looking west across Chapel Ash reveals Compton Road on the left and Tettenhall Road in the centre. The two trams represent the modern face of the town: car 9, one of the original G. F. Milnes double-deckers with reversed staircases, is travelling towards Tettenhall, while car 28, a later Milnes design which, although similar, had a direct, or anti-clockwise, staircase, is working into Wolverhampton. All the other vehicles are horse-drawn, with four two-wheeled carts and, in front of the Regency Westbourne Place, a Hackney Carriage drivers' shelter, with a four-wheeled carriage parked just behind the horse-trough. On the right, the corner site is occupied by Godsell's the chemist, which was later owned by the more famous Boots chain. The residents of the tree-lined Tettenhall Road were instrumental in objecting to the electric tramway with its usual 'unsightly' overhead. As a result of this, and the influence of Alderman Charles Mander, the Lorain Surface Contact system was introduced. If it was not particularly successful, it certainly left everywhere free of overhead wires, enabling the tram routes to retain their uncluttered skyline.

Waiting at the traffic lights at Chapel Ash on 25 September 2000 is Travel West Midlands MCW Metrobus Mk II 3103 (F103 XOF). This 12-year-old, 73-seater double-decker is travelling into the town centre on the 501 service, the Travel West Midlands successor to the old Corporation number 1 trolleybus route, renumbered on 19 May 1976. To the right of the bus is 'Kearneys', a pub that still retains the look of the row of cottages from which it was converted in 1897, while on the right is the late-Victorian block that had included Godsell's; recently this pub has reverted to its older name of the Combermere Arms. The road sign pointing along Tettenhall Road indicates that Thomas Telford's main road to North Wales of the early 1800s is now the A41 and goes to Whitchurch and, appropriately, the 'new town' of Telford. The sign also and somewhat confusingly shows that the road goes to the nearby villages of Perton and Codsall, which were served by Wolverhampton Corporation buses, as well as Tettenhall, the former terminus of both the trams and trolleybuses. Behind the sign is Westbourne Place, which somehow appears far closer to the traffic and somehow less grand and more vulnerable since the reconstruction of the complicated Chapel Ash junction. *J. C. Brown/D. R. Harvey*

Below From outside the Combermere Arms, the view over Chapel Ash looking towards St Mark's Church shows what an important Edwardian suburban centre it was over a century ago. As the lone cyclist travels into town, tramcar 20, one of the 19-24 class of open-top double-deckers built by ER&TCW in 1904, waits outside the Hackney Carriage cabbies' hut and the small cast-iron urinal in front of it before moving off to the Wergs Road terminus at the far end of Upper Green, Tettenhall. It is loading up next to a group of horse-drawn cabs and carriages that are waiting for their next hiring. Behind and to the left of the tram is the impressive Lloyds Bank building on the corner of Clifton Street. *Commercial postcard*

Opposite bottom   Once clear of Chapel Ash, Tettenhall Road's development continued throughout the 1830s and early 1840s, a period reflected in the name plaques mounted on the elegant houses and terraced blocks along the southern side, with Palmerston Place and the terraces of Osborne, Lansdowne, Blenheim, Oakland and Peel gracing the road. No 5 Tettenhall Road, in the block originally named Eagle Terrace, was occupied between 1866 and his death in 1909 by the well-known local botanist and geologist John Frazer, whose collection of over 10,000 items was donated to Wolverhampton's Art Gallery and Museum. Once beyond Clarendon Street, the houses belong to the later, more flamboyant Victorian style, with large villas exemplified by those on the left of this picture. The tram, car 23, is one of the five ER&TCW double-deck trams that entered service between August and October 1902, later being dual-equipped for working over the Wolverhampton District tramlines. It is coming up the hill from Halfway House, with the entrance to Larches Lane next to the parked car, while the dog on the right is crossing Middle Vauxhall, one of the three 'Vauxhalls' built at the end of the Regency period. Adjacent to the tram is the late-Victorian 'garden suburb' of Parkdale. The state of the road, covered with mud and the inevitable horse manure, leaves a lot to be desired. The horse pulling the large-wheeled two-seater trap gallops down the gradient following the tram tracks, belying the many apocryphal tales of horses being electrocuted when treading on the Lorain Surface Contact studs that lay between the tram tracks at 10-foot intervals. It was the electro-magnets on the tram that pulled up the subterranean contact and

made it live – nothing on the surface was depressed to make an electric contact! The contact skate and the six pairs of electro-magnets below the tramcars were 12 feet long, and the whole equipment, weighing over a ton, was sufficiently heavy to depress the studs. The parked 1904-built open car has the registration DA 61, which helps to date this view to within a couple of years of that date. *J. C. Brown collection*

Below   The Georgian inn at the junction of Tettenhall Road and Paget Road, on the left, with the wide opening of Albert Road and Riches Street on the right, was called Halfway House, referring to the pub occupying a position exactly 130 miles from both London to the south-east and Holyhead to the north-west on Thomas Telford's route between the capital and the Anglesey packet port for the Irish Mail services. It is also, coincidentally, halfway between Wolverhampton and Tettenhall village. The man sweeping the street with the long-handled broom is near the impressive front door of the pub, which is advertising its bowling green and garden as well as the availability of teas and light refreshments. Coming into Wolverhampton is an open-topped double-decker tram that by this time has been vestibuled. This, coupled with the dress style of the boys and girls, dates this view to between the summer of 1911 and the outbreak of the Great War. The tram is passing beneath the lime and plane trees that had been planted along Tettenhall Road to enhance the suburban nature of this main road. Waiting at the junction on the right is a family with an infant in its pram being fussed over by an older woman who is perhaps the grandmother. *J. C. Brown collection*

Above On 22 June 1962 the former 1948 Commercial Motor Show exhibit, Sunbeam F4 479 (FJW 479), uses its Metro-Vickers 95hp motors to power its way around the small traffic island at the junction of Tettenhall Road and Paget Road, with the tall-gabled Halfway House pub dominating the junction. Paget Road had been for many years a cul-de-sac, but in the late 1950s it was cut through to become a useful link with Compton Road. Still lining Tettenhall Road are the splendid lime and plane trees seen in the previous photograph, although many of the elms succumbed to Dutch elm disease in the 1980s. Behind the trolleybus, crossing Tettenhall Road, is one of the curvaceously styled Austin A40 Somersets, which with their small 1200cc engines always seemed to be underpowered. Despite only having a top speed of 69mph, which was 1mph slower than the first post-war A40 model, during the Somerset's two-year production run 166,063 were built at Longbridge. On the left is a 1964-registered Triumph Herald convertible, while accelerating into Paget Road is a Vauxhall Wyvern EIX model, looking more like a scaled-down 1950 Chevrolet than a product of what had previously been regarded as one of the more staid of General Motors' car subsidiaries. *J. C. Brown*

Below Peak-time operation of works and school services was generally worked by trolleybuses, but obviously they were limited by their overhead; extra motorbus journeys would therefore be slotted into the timetables for those institutions that could command the custom, and the service would start in the road alongside their premises. Although the trolleybuses have been gone for about seven years and the bus is no longer painted in the Corporation livery, the Wolverhampton College of Further Education in Paget Road, which was the main centre for teacher-training in the town, had such a bus service, which had originated during the latter years of the trolleybus route along Tettenhall Road. Freshly repainted in WMPTE livery and waiting for students before dispatching them to town in early 1970 is MCCW-bodied Guy 'Arab' IV 46 (4046 JW), which entered service in October 1961. *P. Roberts*

Opposite top In this winter scene taken in the early 1930s, the sweep of the large Victorian semi-detached villas along Tettenhall Road towards St Jude's Road West and on towards Newbridge stretches beyond the two small lorries to the left of the trolleybus. Behind the trees on the right is the C of E Church of St Jude, while opposite the four girls begin their journey home, wearing the smart blue

uniform of Wolverhampton Girls' High School, having walked the short distance from the school drive to the Paget Road junction in the foreground. The Girls' School opened in 1911 and thrives today as a Grant Maintained Grammar School. Opposite the girls is the broad junction of Albert Road and Riches Street. The latter, leading to Whitmore Reans, still has its original nameplate on the stone wall, and was named after John Riches, the local Secretary of the Freehold Land Society, which was affiliated to the 1820s Chartist Movement. The Chartists were heavily involved in buying plots of land for working men in order for them to become self-sufficient in their own produce and to enable them to construct their own house on their own land. The most famous local example of such a scheme is to be found in the village of Dodford, near Bromsgrove, set up in the 1830s by the Chartists as a model community whose livelihood

centred upon their collective strawberry-growing. The origins of Albert Road are more prosaic, being named, like many a road throughout the country, after Queen Victoria's Consort. The trolleybus is one of the 62-66 batch of Guy BTXs fitted with Dodson H30/31R bodies, and the first trolleybuses in the fleet to have a single-step entrance to the rear platform. Despite having modern-looking rear ends, their frontal appearance was positively archaic! The upper saloon was set back level with the lower saloon front bulkhead, and was a design that Dodson developed for the independent 'Pirate' operators in London, usually mounted on Leyland 'Titan' TD1 motorbus chassis. This batch could be distinguished by their five-bay construction and the deep-yellow-painted waistrail below the lower saloon windows. They were delivered in January and February 1930 and differed from the next batch, which, although having the same combination of chassis and bodybuilder, were of the older style of six-bay construction. *Bennett Clarke*

Above right Looking from St Jude's Road West back towards the Halfway House public house, just visible in the distance,

reveals how attractively laid out was this arborially rich area. Open-top G. F. Milnes reverse-staircase tramcar 9 trundles into Wolverhampton in the latter part of the Edwardian decade without another vehicle in sight. It is passing St Jude's Church on Tettenhall Road, which was consecrated on 20 April 1869, having been heavily subsidised by a Miss Mary Stokes. Her religious philanthropy helped to produce this attractively Gothic-styled church, the well-proportioned tower of which, surmounted by a spire, was designed by an architect called Bidlake, and was one of the better-looking Victorian churches in the town. Tettenhall Road's wide-open character, lined with what even in the late 1880s, when they were built, were expensive semi-detached villas, was unique in Wolverhampton. Practically every large town and city in the United Kingdom has its most expensive houses to the west of the town centre; this is because these areas got the clean, unpolluted air from the prevailing winds, which by the time it reached the 'east end' of town had been contaminated by smoke and soot from the local factories. Wolverhampton's Tettenhall Road, leading to the west, fitted this urban model perfectly. *J. C. Brown collection*

Left On 4 August 1962, approaching the south end of Newbridge Crescent where it meets Tettenhall Road, is Roe-rebodied Sunbeam W4 trolleybus 431 (DUK 831). This trolleybus re-entered service with its new body on 18 November 1958 and is nearing its first Corporation repaint the following November. It is passing a 1956 Worcestershire-registered Austin A50 Cambridge, which appears to be in trouble with a punctured rear tyre. Following the trolleybus are two of the very popular Ford 100E series cars, the nearer one being an Anglia and behind it the equivalent four-door Prefect model. Just to the right of the Standard Atlas van and also travelling out of the town centre is an early example of the famous Volkswagen 'Beetle'. *J. C. Brown*

Below left Four young lads stand facing the photographer at a time when anyone photographing street scenes attracted attention. In this Edwardian view, tramcar 27, one of the 25-30 batch of direct-staircase double-deckers built by G. F. Milnes in 1904, stands at the junction with New Hampton Road West; it is displaying an advertisement on its balcony panel for Allen's Pianos. Alongside it is a row of 16 bay-windowed terraced houses dating from the 1890s, and immediately beyond them, where the tall trees hang over the road, is the former entrance to the Wolverhampton Tramways horse-tram depot, next to the York Hotel. Newbridge depot was finally sold in 1911 to a Mr A. Wilkes and to the Wolverhampton Electricity Department. In the distance, beyond the tram coming towards Newbridge, can just be made out the spire of St Jude's Church. Although this is about 1907, the only other vehicles in Tettenhall Road are horse-drawn. Just visible in the road opposite the tram power section box, alongside the four boys, is the track junction with New Hampton Road West; this section of

track was not normally used for passenger services, but enabled the transfer of tramcars between Whitmore Reans and West Park and the 'main-road' Tettenhall Road service. By the time the 2 and 7 trolleybus service to Whitmore Reans was introduced on 27 January 1930, this section of New Hampton Road had long been devoid of any public passenger transport service. *J. Hughes collection*

Below Guy BT trolleybus 651 (FJW 651) approaches the same junction from the opposite direction on 1 September 1961, when it seemed unimaginable that just 22 months later Tettenhall Road would be left to the tender mercies of the diesel-engined bus. Although the use of overhead electricity supply had been a *cause célèbre* in the town, Tettenhall Road was perhaps the best example, where mature trees successfully masked its presence. But while the overhead may have been on the debit side, the 'silent service' provided trolleybuses at a 6 to 8-minute frequency. At its best, the Tettenhall trolleybus service was the 'jewel in the crown' in terms of the area through which it ran. This Park Royal-bodied trolleybus is passing the grounds of Newbridge House, which can be glimpsed above the Keep Left bollard on the right. No 651 had been repaired only a year earlier after being involved in a bad accident at Eve Hill, Dudley, in August 1960. The mock-half-timbered building to the right of the trolleybus is The Newbridge public house; opened in 1938, it replaced a Georgian single-storey building on the other side of the road that had been built at about the same time as the completion of the Staffordshire & Worcester Canal. Behind the trolleybus is a petrol station that was contemporary with the pre-war reconstruction of the Tettenhall Road bridge through Newbridge. *J. C. Brown*

Above Seen from approximately the same position as the previous photograph, two of the earliest electric trams purchased by the Corporation are standing near where the horse-trams terminated at Newbridge between 1878 and 1902. No 11, the double-decker, is one of the G. F. Milnes cars delivered in May 1902 and mounted on Lorain-DuPont trucks with two 25hp Lorain motors. It was also one of the first trams to be top-covered in 1911. Standing next to it is car 10, an unusual type of single-deck open combination tram also built by Milnes and again mounted on the heavyweight Lorain-DuPont trucks. Although both were delivered for the opening of the experimental mile-long Lorain Surface Contact system in Bilston Road on 6 February 1902, the single-decker was indeed a strange tram for a municipality to purchase. It had an enclosed central saloon for 16 passengers and an open cross-bench at both ends on either side of the main bulkheads for four rows of passengers, making it possible for eight people to sit in the open. Wolverhampton purchased four such tramcars (2, 4, 7 and 10), but it was not really surprising that no further examples were purchased. The quartet had this open section closed in, making them look like normal single-deckers. In the foreground the rarely used tram tracks curve round into New Hampton Road West, while in the distance the pony and trap and the second double-decker tram are passing the northern end of Newbridge Crescent; beyond again is the straight section of

road bridge over the canal and Smestow Brook. *J. Hughes collection*

Opposite bottom In September 1901 the construction of the Lorain tram tracks is under way at Newbridge, having begun on 20 May when Alderman Charles Mander ceremonially 'broke the ground' in New Hampton Road West near Tettenhall Road. The existing horse-tram service was gradually more and more disrupted on the Wolverhampton side of the boundary, while the councillors in Tettenhall held a series of meetings, culminating on 8 August 1901, concerning the construction of the extension into The Rock, the steep section of Tettenhall Road climbing from Newbridge out of the Smestow Valley and up into Tettenhall. Within a few weeks, construction and operating agreements having been confirmed, work began in Newbridge on the Tettenhall side of the boundary, concentrating on the north side of the road as it was deemed undesirable to disturb the public utilities, especially the main gas pipe, that lay on the south side. On the left is one of the UDC's gas street lamps, while behind the trees is a large area of open parkland. The block of Victorian shops on the extreme right survive to the present day, and are an excellent marker as to where this track-laying was taking place. What is interesting is just how labour-intensive were such civil engineering schemes – at least 17 men armed with only picks, shovels, crowbars and wheelbarrows are involved. At this stage only the tracks have been laid, with the Lorain contact stud infrastructure yet to be installed The whole operation has attracted the usual onlookers of young boys and families. *J. C. Brown collection*

This page Standing at the Newbridge terminus opposite Newbridge Crescent during the early part of 1900 is horse-tram 24; it would not be long before the Wolverhampton Tramways Company was taken over by the Corporation on 1 May of that year. The terminus of this standard gauge, 1 mile 5 furlong line was near the Wolverhampton CBC/Tettenhall UDC boundary opposite the north end of Newbridge Crescent, a point that had been the terminus since the opening of the line on 1 May 1878. Unusually, the wrought iron tram tracks had a central groove, to the patents of Mr Joseph Kincaid, while the 43lb per yard rails had a serrated inner surface, which helped the horses get a better grip. The tram, which was one of four extra cars required for the increase in traffic that occurred at this time, would be about eight years old, having been built in 1892 by the Falcon Engine & Car Works of Loughborough at a cost of about £200 each. These 44-seater double-deckers were based at Newbridge Depot for use on the Tettenhall Road service. The two horses were named Dick and Diana, while

Mr J. Bruerton was the driver, and standing in the road is Mr H. Icke, the conductor.

A Wolverhampton Tramways Company standard-gauge horse-tram is preserved at the Black Country Living Museum, Dudley. Car 23, sister tram to 24 seen above, was restored by the British Horse Tram Enthusiasts Society, and suddenly brings to life the flat, century-old sepia-toned black and white photographs, bringing the realisation that the Victorian world was not dark, depressing and grey but had brightly coloured vehicles such as this. These six-windowed Tramways Company vehicles were painted in crimson and yellow with white window surrounds and corner posts, and had a garden-seat layout on the top deck. With the exception of their trucks and obviously their method of propulsion, they were very similar to the first electric tramcars supplied to other operators in the country. Several Corporations, including Glasgow and Belfast, converted their very similar horse-trams to electric propulsion. Standing behind the horse-tram in the replica Hawthorns tram depot is Wolverhampton Corporation electric tram 49, built by UEC in 1909 for the final Lorain extension on the system along Lea Road. *Bennett Clarke/D. R. Harvey*

Above Brindley's original bridge over his Staffordshire & Worcestershire Canal was completed in 1772, but the area had been known as New Bridge well before that date, presumably referring to the river bridge over Smestow Brook. The second bridge dated from the improvements to the Wolverhampton Turnpike undertaken by Thomas Telford, whose 'Holyhead Road' was commissioned by Parliament in 1808 and completed in 1828, the section across the Smestow Valley and up the hill to Upper Green via The Rock being completed in about 1824. Telford's bridge, with the Newbridge Inn of a similar age to Brindley's canal, were in turn swept away in the spring of 1937, and a new structure over both the river and the canal was ready for traffic in the months immediately before the outbreak of the Second World War. The incorporation of the former GWR line into the concept was undertaken by the Borough Engineer, who not only designed a bridge that was more than 30 yards long, but also wide enough to be included in a scheme for making Tettenhall Road into a dual carriageway. Trolleybus 602 (FJW 602), a Park Royal-bodied Guy BT that entered service on 28 September 1949, stands at the bus stop on the wide section of the bridge on 4 August 1962. Just five weeks later it would be prematurely withdrawn after an accident on the Dudley service on 11 September. It is being overtaken by an MG Magnette ZA saloon and an J2 van. Behind the MG is a row of cottages dating from the middle of the 19th century, with gable-end advertisements for Wall's Ice Cream and Mackeson stout. Passing these buildings, roughly where the petrol filling station was situated, is a 'Mr Whippy' ice-cream van. *J. C. Brown*

Below left Perhaps the most spectacular accident on the trolleybus system occurred at Tettenhall Road, Newbridge, on 22 May 1946. Trolleybus 295 (DDA 995) skidded on its way from Tettenhall into town, and was left teetering over the embankment that led down to the railway line some 30 feet below. It was a Sunbeam MF2 fitted with one of the last non-'austerity'-style Charles Roe H29/25R bodies built by the Leeds-based bodybuilder to full pre-war specification. It was Wolverhampton's last 'pre-war' vehicle, actually entering service on 4 April 1942. No 295 is seen pointing nose-first down the bank with its trolleybooms pointing limply skywards and its cab door open, from which Driver Hubbard jumped out to help Conductor Cahill assist the ten passengers from the stricken vehicle. It was recovered during the following day, using two of Pat Collins Circus's Burrell steam traction engines, *Mabon* and *Goliath*, and returned to service soon afterwards, being relatively unscathed by its attempt to do 'a triple somersault with pike and two tucks' from the 'top board' on to the railway line. Within six months, on 22 November, it had turned over in Bradmore Road at Bantock Park – if a bus had a death wish it was this one! Eventually 295 was sold to Belfast Corporation on 23 May 1952 at the bargain price of just £150, becoming their 245 and lasting only until June 1954. *D. R. Harvey collection*

Opposite top An unidentified open-topped tramcar is travelling over the single-line section of track in The Rock some time after 1911, as it is vestibuled. This 1 in 22 gradient was never climbed by the horse-trams, and even in electric days proved a severe challenge, especially when the tramcar was full. On the right, half-way up the hill, is an elegant, late-Georgian house, while on the left the nearest cottage belongs to E. J. Adey, who 'repairs, hires and sells cycles'; some of his wares are propped up outside his converted house. Next door, the last building before the trees take over this sandstone cutting is the builder's yard of R. W. Foxhall, a converted farmyard barn. *J. C. Brown*

Centre and bottom At the top of the climb up The Rock, through the picturesque archway of trees, Tettenhall Road emerges at the junction with Stockwell Road on the left and Upper Green on the right. Coming out of Stockwell Road is a Bedford A5-type lorry belonging to Collins Parcel Service Ltd, while on the right, beyond the mound surmounted by a Clock Tower commemorating the Coronation of King George V on 22 June 1911 and donated by Mr & Mrs Edward Swindley, is a Hillman Husky. At this junction Tettenhall Road becomes Wergs Road and very quickly becomes lined with some very attractive, expensive but strangely dated 1960s detached houses. Emerging from the arboreal gloom of The Rock on 1 September 1961 is Park Royal-bodied Guy BT trolleybus 635 (FJW 635) on its way to the terminus of the 1 route. Above the cutting on the left is one of the mock-Tudor Victorian-built houses that lined Stockwell Road and gave this part of Tettenhall the look of a village.

The lime, sycamore and plane trees have for many years provided this delightful tunnel of foliage on the climb up from Newbridge. On 25 September 2000 at about 3.30pm on a normal Monday, what had previously been a scene full of traffic at the top of The Rock quite suddenly became totally deserted. The writer had been waiting patiently to recreate the previous photograph when from deep within the dark canopy of trees came the unmistakable rumbling of a Gardner 6LXB engine in third gear, powering a double-decker up the hill. There was still not another vehicle in sight as MCW 'Metrobus' Mk II 3103 (F103 XOF) emerged with a roar from the gloom like a railway locomotive from a tunnel, crossed the box junction and pulled up at the stop at Upper Green. The busy scene of 1961 had provided a lot of noisy traffic and a silent trolleybus, a strange contrast to the unusually empty road of 2000. *J. C. Brown/D. R. Harvey*

Left It is 1 September 1961 and the girl at the zebra crossing, in her summer frock and canvas plimsolls, will have only another two or three days left of her summer holiday before she will have to return for the start of a new year at school. With her mother and infant sibling in the pram, she is waiting for the empty Carrimore car-transporter powered by an Austin FF tractor unit to overtake the stationary trolleybus and hopefully stop to enable them to cross the road towards the inviting paddling pool in which are playing a large number of children. Following the transporter is a two-tone Standard Vanguard Luxury Six, while in the distance, near the trolleybus terminus, is a Ford Anglia 105E with its distinctive raked-back rear window. The trolleybus is 629 (FJW 629), Wolverhampton's penultimate Sunbeam F4. It entered service on 2 May 1950 and was withdrawn when not 12 years old on 28 February 1962, being one of four F4s and two Guy BTs that were due for overhaul and were surplus to requirements. It has left the terminus at Tettenhall and travelled the short distance to park next to the substantial yet rustic bus stop in Upper Green near the corner of Stockwell Road. *J. C. Brown*

Below left The wide turning circle at the terminus of the Tettenhall trolleybus route was in the naturally wide 'throat' of the junction of the main Wergs Road (the A41) with Wrottesley Road. The Thomas Telford-designed 'Holyhead Road' from this point onwards is characterised by limestone walls, a feature found only north and west of Sedgley. Behind the turning motorbus is a large Victorian house overlooking the road junction with its attic 'look-out' window. Trolleybuses dominated Wolverhampton's 'main-road' routes, and the Tettenhall Road route was no exception, so it is unusual to see anything other than a trolleybus during that era. Turning beneath the trolleybus turning loop wires on a rainy day in April 1962 is 519 (FJW 519), a Daimler CVG6 with a Brush H29/25R body that had entered service

in February 1950 and would survive until near the end of 1969 in WMPTE ownership. On careful examination is turns out not to be in revenue-earning service, but is on a driver route-learning run. The blind in the destination box has been turned to a white blank display, which is less helpful even than 'SPECIAL'. As the trolleybuses were not abandoned until 30 June 1963, it is unlikely that the bus is being used in connection with that change-over. On the extreme left is the mock-Elizabethan-fronted Mitchells & Butlers-owned Dog & Gun public house. On the right Wergs Road, with its highly prosperous housing, is a continuation of Upper Green, becoming better known as the A41 to Whitchurch and Chester. *S. R. Dewey*

Below The first production batch of double-decker trolleybuses, after the success of the open-staircase prototype Guy BTX, were seven similar vehicles numbered 34-40, but this time their Christopher Dodson bodies were fitted with enclosed staircases. They were quite massive for their time, seating 33 in the upper saloon and 28 in the lower and weighing a shade over 6½ tons. At the turning circle inside Wrottesley Road and about to be manoeuvred round to the stop at the Tettenhall terminus is 35 (UK 635), which entered service on 11 July 1927, the same day as the Penn Fields 4 route was opened. Standing on the platform while his colleague in the cab hauls the heavy-steering trolleybus around is the conductor wearing his Bell Punch ticket machine and his rack of tickets. In this winter scene the trolleybus has just passed a steam road-roller, puffing up and down a short section of road at the edge of Upper Green, Wergs Road. It is being employed on road repairs, but in the early 1930s there was insufficient traffic to require the use of that scourge of the present day, the dreaded temporary traffic lights! In front of the trolleybus on the left is a sign at the edge of the open land in Wergs Road that reads 'To the Wolverhampton Rugby Union Football Club'. *J. Hughes collection*

Above The opening of the tram route to West Park for the Wolverhampton Art & Industrial Exhibition took place on 1 May 1902 using the line along New Hampton Road East as far as Coleman Street. Although a double-track triangular junction at Tettenhall Road was laid during 1901, the trams reached Newbridge for the first time by way of the 'main-road' route along Tettenhall Road, opened on 12 June 1902, and the link from Coleman Street along New Hampton Road was only inaugurated on 11 August 1902. By the time the extension up the steep hill at The Rock and on to Upper Green, Tettenhall, was ready for traffic on 13 September, the Exhibition was approaching the end of its six-month duration. The Wergs Road terminus at the western end of Upper Green was an extremely exposed point, especially in inclement weather. After numerous meetings and petitions from Tettenhall residents, the Swiss Chalet from the West Park Exhibition was re-erected opposite the drinking fountain in March 1903. Amazingly, this wooden structure survived until 1972, by which time the ravages of the elements and many years of neglect had taken their toll.

Several attempts were made to retain it, but when it was demolished it almost fell down. Yet it was a strange link with the 1902 Exhibition, outlasting the trams, the trolleybuses and even municipal transport operation in Wolverhampton. Tram 26, one of the last Milnes-built trams of 1904, stands at the Swiss Chalet terminus in about 1907. This photograph was taken by a Mr Hart, who was assistant to the well-known Wolverhampton photographer Bennett Clark. The film used at the time was unable to pick up yellow, so Wolverhampton's tramcars always look as though they are in a colour scheme of 'dark and dingy', which did not reflect their true bright olive green and gamboge yellow livery. *J. Hughes collection*

Below By the early 1960s the Swiss Chalet, seen in a dilapidated condition behind the trolleybus, was beginning to show its age after many years of neglect. Awaiting departure time at the attractive 1 route terminus in Wergs Road, the trolleybus conductor talks to the driver in the cab of Park Royal-bodied Sunbeam F4 624 (FJW 624), which entered service on 25 March 1950 and remained in traffic until the

closure of the Penn and Penn Fields trolleybus routes on 9 June 1963. These Sunbeams, and the virtually identical and contemporary Guy BTs, were the mainstay of the Tettenhall Road trolleybus service from their introduction between 1948 and 1950 until the Tettenhall service was abandoned on 30 June 1963. Although the Roe-rebodied Sunbeam W4s were also used on the route, these 8-feet-wide trolleybuses were used on the all-day service until the end. There was always an impression that the most recently repainted vehicles were used on this service, giving credence to the notion that this route was Wolverhampton's 'Premier Line'. *J. C. Brown*

Top In the years between the trolleybus abandonment in 1963 and the take-over of the Corporation's buses by the WMPTE in October

1969, the 1 bus route was operated initially by UK-registered Weymann-bodied Guy 'Arab' Vs, which had reverted to a half-cab layout. By this time the pagoda-towered Tettenhall terminus shelter is displaying its advancing years in a yet more careworn, yet genteel, manner, still able to reflect its once imposing Edwardian grandeur. The rider of the moped speeds past the shelter and the leafless trees on his way across Upper Green towards the green-and-yellow-painted Corporation double-decker standing in the bus lay-by at the 1 route terminus. In the spring of 1967 these Guys would themselves be replaced by single-deck Strachan-bodied, dual-door AEC 'Swifts' and Daimler 'Roadliners', put on to the 1 route on 12 June 1967. However, they lasted for barely six weeks before being transferred to the country routes, whereupon the Tettenhall service reverted to double-decker operation. *D. R. Harvey collection*

Above right Attractive double-decker 365 (DJW 765) seems to have gone for a ride into the countryside and, having reversed through a gate into a field deep in rural Staffordshire, is having a quiet rest in the sun. In fact,

because of roadworks in the village during June 1955, it is just beyond the normal 51 route terminus at Wergs, in a lane nearly opposite Wrottesley Park, on the main A41 road. It was at Wrottesley Park that Queen Wilhemina of the Netherlands reviewed her Dutch troops prior to the D-Day invasion of France in May 1944. The bus is a wartime Guy 'Arab' II, its chassis dating from 1943; it was rebodied by Charles Roe in 1951 with an H31/25R body, one of 20 'Arab' IIs rebodied at about that time. Roe, a comparatively rare supplier of bodies to operators in the West Midlands, also at this time rebodied 17 pre-war and wartime Daimler chassis for Coventry Corporation, using the same style. The rebodied Wolverhampton Guys gave another ten years of useful revenue-earning service, which was perhaps a little surprising as they had the bus's normal somewhat difficult and unforgiving crash gearbox, whereas the Corporation had standardised on an 'easy-change' fleet of motorbuses since 1934. The new bus body was equipped with the usual Roe features, including the Patent Safety Staircase and characteristic teak rubbing strip below the lower saloon windows. *J. C. Brown*

Top The outer terminus of the Wednesday-and-Saturday-only 27 service to Beckbury was opposite the church alongside a farmyard with a well-ventilated brick barn. In 1964 551 (FJW 551), a Guy 'Arab' III 6LW with a Park Royal 54-seater body, waits at the stop. Despite its slightly dated appearance, it entered service in October 1950, and is working on a route inherited from Midland Red in 1928, having been inaugurated on 9 May 1925 by that company; the bus would survive to see service with the WMPTE until 1970. Its crew is waiting for the rush of passengers, who just might be the couple strolling along the lane towards the bus.

Despite its distance from even the outpost of Wergs, well beyond the Tettenhall trolleybus terminus, the service from Beckbury back to Wolverhampton by way of Burnhill Green and Boningale took 44 minutes. There were three buses each way on Tuesdays and Fridays, four round trips on Wednesdays and Saturdays, and two journeys on Sunday afternoons. *D. Nicholson*

Middle To reach the village of Tong Norton the bus travelled along the A41 from Wolverhampton via Tettenhall, Kingswood, Albrighton, Cosford and Tong and finally to the Bell Inn at Tong Norton. Although about to be transferred to Midland Red three days later, former Corporation 719 (NJW 719E), a Strachan dual-door-bodied Daimler 'Roadliner' SRC6, by now repainted in West Midlands PTE blue and cream livery, lies over opposite the Bell Inn in Tong Norton village on 1 December 1973. These single-deckers were hamstrung by their appallingly unsuitable American-designed Cummins V6-200 9.63-litre engines. Although very compact, which advantageously allowed an extremely gently ramped floor towards the rear of the bus, the engine was terribly noisy, vibrated and rattled, wouldn't start when hot, was unreliable and made clouds of black smoke when starting. That, coupled with the Corporation's choice of distinctly fragile Strachan bodies on the six Daimler 'Roadliner' SRC6s, as well as another six identical bodies on the equally unreliable AEC 'Swift' MP2Rs chassis, meant that all of these single-deckers were taken out of service by West Midlands PTE between 1971 and 1974, with 719 surviving until the end of 1974 and subsequently becoming one of the prized preserved exhibits at the B&MMOT bus museum at Wythall. *R. Smith*

Bottom The 49 bus service to Albrighton and Tong was extended on Wednesdays and Saturdays to Offoxey Farm, with a total journey time of 50 minutes; it also served the RAF station at Cosford. The terminus at the top of the hill at Offoxey village was reached by little more than a lane, and it is up this steep rise from nearby Tong Norton that Wolverhampton's only 'standard' (if there was such a thing) Guy 'Wulfrunian' is climbing. It is, however, a bit of a cheat as this is an Omnibus Society tour to some of Wolverhampton Corporation's country outposts, but it does show that these services were genuinely 'country'. The 'Wulfrunian', with its large-capacity East Lancashire front-entrance body, was never a great success in normal revenue service, although it was used for enthusiasts' tours because of its rarity value. It was withdrawn in 1970 and languished for well over a year until being sold eventually to Wombwell Diesels in March 1972. *D. Nicholson*

Whitmore Reans

The Victorian suburb of Whitmore Reans was developed in the 1850s as a superior urban development to the north of Tettenhall Road. Originally named New Hampton to convey the right impression, it was located about a mile to the north-west of the town centre, and was reached by travelling out of the town centre by way of Wulfruna Street and passing the Market Place before reaching the appalling houses in North Street, which dated from the early 17th century. Wolverhampton was a 'midden' town, which meant that it had no mains drainage, and this way out of the town was at first as bad as any other. Passing Gifford House, an early Georgian house that was a disguised Roman Catholic Church, the way went down the steep west-facing Wadham's Hill and Whitmore Hill, which because of their exposure were considered suitable locations for the emerging industrial bourgeoisie of the town to build their houses. This west aspect had the advantage of facing away from the pollution, in an area where the cost of the fresh air was only affordable by the wealthy.

Once the flat land was reached, the upwardly mobile Victorians had obvious pretensions, as not only was the main road called New Hampton Road, but also the five-way road junction, where originally a number of field boundaries met, was named Leicester Square. The area grew throughout the 1860s, adding churches, schools and shops to the housing of the suburb, although by the time the 50-acre West Park was opened on Whit Monday, 6 June 1881, some of the newer housing was more artisan than the earlier villa types. West Park cost £16,000 and was situated on a 'treeless swamp' lying between New Hampton Road and Tettenhall Road; it included a clock tower, an ornamental fountain and a large lake, and was known as 'The People's Park'. The most significant event to be held at West Park was the Arts & Industrial Exhibition, which, with its veritable Crystal Palace of steel and glass conservatories, concert halls and industrial displays, was destined to lose the town over £30,000. But it began the greening of Wolverhampton and started a new era of social facilities in the town, and in 2002 has been expensively restored to its Victorian splendour.

The effect of this event on Whitmore Reans was to be dramatic as far as public transport was concerned. The Corporation was extremely resolute about the construction and opening of its third Lorain Surface Contact electric tram route to Whitmore Reans in order to serve the prestigious opening of the Arts & Industrial on 1 May 1902. With the three original trams (10-12), bought for the experimental service between Cleveland Road and Ettingshall Road that had opened on 6 February 1902, together with a further nine (1-9), the new electric tram service was opened on time from Victoria Square to Coleman Street to serve the exhibition. On 11 August 1902 the route was extended along New Hampton Road West to join up with the Tettenhall service at Newbridge, which had opened on 12 June of that year. However, after 30 October 1903 the passenger part of the service from Leicester Square to Newbridge was cut back, with the section down to Newbridge being retained as the only place on the system where a tram could be turned round. Following public and press pressure, the service along New Hampton Road was extended once more to Hunter Street, and this situation lasted until the conversion of the route from the Lorain system to the overhead method of current collection. This occurred on 28 August 1921, when the Whitmore Reans tram route became the fifth service to be converted. The section from Hunter Street along New Hampton Road West to the Tettenhall junction at Newbridge was never wired, although the turning triangle was. This situation only lasted until 1 October 1927, when the trams ceased running, being replaced by large-capacity six-wheeled double-decker motorbuses. The bus route was extended into Court Road and Hordern Road, forming a circular service around the Whitmore Reans suburb, and lasted until the buses were replaced by trolleybuses on 27 January 1930.

The description of the subsequent trolleybus developments and the associated bus services to Blakeley Green and Codsall will be included in Part 3, when the Whitmore Reans trolleybus route was tied in with the cross-town route to Darlaston.

Below Taking the development of a basic Edwardian double-decker about as far as it could go on Wolverhampton's 3ft 6in gauge tracks is car 18. This tram, the last of a second batch of nine, was delivered in August 1902 by G. F. Milnes as an open-topped car, with reversed stairs and mounted on Lorain DuPont trucks for use over the American-designed Lorain Surface Contact stud system. Car 18 had a seating capacity of 22 inside and 26 'up top', which was destined not to alter. However, everything else about the tramcar did – it was fitted with an enclosed vestibule in the 1911-12 period to improve the health of the motormen. Subsequently top-covered, the open balcony was a reminder that the Board of Trade would not sanction totally enclosed four-wheeled double-decker trams on 3ft 6in gauge tracks. This did not prevent Birmingham Corporation Tramways from operating two, Walsall six, and South Staffordshire Tramways having car 34, an experimental one-man tram. Finally, car 18 was equipped with a trolleypole when the Lorain system was abandoned

during 1921. It is seen here in its final condition in about 1926, standing in Victoria Square having worked in from Whitmore Reans. Behind is one of the non-covered trams, while to the right are hoardings advertising a wide range of beverages including Oxo, Camp coffee, Bovril and Bass beer, while the Scala Cinema in Worcester Street is showing the silent film *Peter the Great*. *R. Wilson*

Bottom left The unique Tilling-Stevens TS15A stands in Victoria Square at the Sir Tatton Sykes public house when working on the Whitmore Reans service. The trams stopped working on this route on 1 October 1927, and it was during the interregnum before trolleybuses were introduced on 27 January 1930 that motorbuses were employed on the service. Wolverhampton Corporation managed, over a period of about eight years, to acquire some of the real 'lost causes' in the PSV market, including an AJS 'Commodore', four Sunbeam 'Pathans', the only Sunbeam DF2 double-decker ever built, and two single-decker and one double-decker pre-war Guy 'Arabs'. If there was a bigger 'turkey' to purchase, however, it was the Tilling-Stevens TS15A, which entered service with its 66-seater enclosed-staircase Christopher Dodson body in 1928. Numbered 66 in the bus fleet with the registration UK 5366, this impressive 30-foot-long six-wheeler had only a 36.5hp four-cylinder engine, which meant that it was less powerful than the preceding Guy CXs. This was one of the Tilling-Stevens company's last attempt to persevere with petrol-electric transmission, and although the bus's chassis was exhibited at the 1927 Commercial Motor Show at Olympia, it seems to have been the only one to have entered service anywhere! Its career in Wolverhampton was fairly quiet, for this 'leviathan'

disappeared about 1931, turning up as a showman's lorry in Birmingham with a conventional gearbox. *J. Cooper*

Below ER&TCW double-deck tram 3, mounted on a Brill 21E truck, is boarded by two young women in Princes Square in early 1904, while working on the Whitmore Reans service after the closure of the West Park Show. The Coleman Street destination was discontinued when the Whitmore Reans service was extended once more along New Hampton Road West as far as Hunter Street on 26 January 1905. The open-topper, with its impressive upper saloon lights, stands at the 'All Cars Stop Here' sign protected by four decorative bollards, which look more akin to the horse posts of 50 years earlier. Just above the tram stop sign is an early reminder to other road users to 'Keep To The Left'. In later years this location would become the site of the first electrically operated traffic lights in the United Kingdom. To the right is the corner block containing the impressive Price Lewis clothes shop, better known as the Royal London Mutual Insurance Society building; this was still fairly new, having been opened only two years earlier. Beyond, in Lichfield Street, the new bank for the London, City & Metropolitan has not yet been built, as the old 18th-century block is still being used.

The canopies on the left belong to a splendid late-Victorian 'pile' whose ground floor is occupied by Bradley's toy shop, but this would later become the premises of the Westminster Bank. Alas, the canopies, with their wrought iron columns and panelled glass roof, did not survive long into the new century. Unfortunately, the original glass negative also failed to survive intact, hence the missing section in the top left-hand corner. *J. Hughes collection*

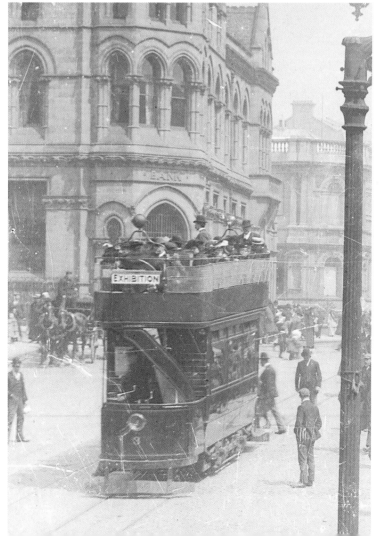

Above Vestibuled tramcar 50 travels along Lichfield Street toward Queen Square in June 1919 when working on the Whitmore Reans route. It is passing the impressive Italian-styled Museum & Art Gallery, opened in 1885, which was paid for surreptitiously by Philip Horsman, a local builder; his covert philanthropy was eventually discovered and to the right of the tram is the Horsman Fountain. Car 50 was built by the United Electric Car Co on Brill 21E trucks with 51 seats, and entered service in 1913. This was a very significant Wolverhampton tramcar as it was the first in the fleet to have a top-cover and to have enclosed vestibules, with triangular dash panels. Following the tram is a Midland Red Brush-bodied Tilling-Stevens TS3 single-decker, which is passing the impressive Gothic-styled Barclays Bank building, opened in 1876 to the designs of T. H. Fleeming. On the extreme right, next to the Art Gallery & Museum, are the impressive columns of the London, City & Metropolitan Bank. *D. R. Harvey collection*

Left The electric tramcar route operated to serve the West Park Arts & Industrial Exhibition, opened on 1 May 1902 and boasting a concert hall, industrial displays, a hall of laughter, the first spiral toboggan in the country, and a collection of huge glasshouses; however, it was very poorly attended and lost the Corporation more than £30,000. Even the opening of the New Hampton Road tram service on the same day as the great Edwardian

extravaganza failed to entice the public in the hoped-for numbers. Initially the service ran as far as Coleman Street, but was extended to Newbridge on 11 August 1902, enabling the service to West Park to become linked to the Wergs Road, Tettenhall, route. Car 3, constructed by ER&TCW as an open-topped, 48-seater double-decker, is passing through Queen Square during the five months that this Exhibition service operated, with the impressive Barclays Bank towering over it. Carrying the destination 'EXHIBITION', it entered service in May 1902 and was first used on the New Hampton Road service. Car 3 and double-decker tram 9, a G. F. Milnes-built vehicle, were the only early double-deckers fitted with Brill 21E trucks and working on the Lorain Surface Contact system. *O. Wildsmith*

Above Trundling down Waterloo Road from Darlington Street in about 1910 is Wolverhampton Corporation tramcar 27. Built by the G. F. Milnes Company of Hadley, Shrewsbury, as an open-topper with a direct staircase and Brill 21E truck, it was one of the 25-30 class that entered service at the beginning of 1904. The first four of the class, including car 27, re-entered service with trolleypoles on 9 November 1905 in order to allow through running on the

Stow Heath Lane to Bilston stretch of the Wolverhampton District Electric Tramways overhead-powered line. The Whitmore Reans tram route was powered at this time by the Lorain Surface Contact stud system, and the studs between the tracks can just be made out to the left of the trotting horse pulling the two-wheeled trap; as a result, dual-equipped car 27 is running with its trolleypole tied down. The fact that horses and the studs lived in such close proximity rather belies the apocryphal stories of horses being electrocuted when they stood on the contact stud!

The horse and trap are passing the uncertainly styled Baptist Church, which was opened in 1901; over the next 50 years the Rev Leslie Chown was the only minister, still being an active preacher well into his late 80s. The building behind the tramcar is the Darlington Street Methodist Church, which, with its unusual central dome, was designed by Arthur Marshall and opened on 29 October 1901, having replaced a far more gracious building that dated from 1825. The tree-lined Waterloo Road, prior to the Great War, was a prestigious address and contained some attractively stuccoed terraces of circa 1840-50, whose style was still intrinsically Regency. A number of these, covered in ivy, stand next to the Baptist Church. *J. Hughes collection*

Above The conversion of the Whitmore Reans tram route from the increasingly unreliable and expensive to maintain Lorain stud pick-up system to the normal overhead electrical collection method took place on 28 August 1921. During the summer of 1923, soon after the conversion, car 15, a double-decker tram built by G. F. Milnes, originally open-topped but now with an enclosed upper saloon and enclosed vestibule platforms, passes townwards along New Hampton Road East and begins the climb up to the junction with Waterloo Road. The houses on the left, with their bay windows, attics and small walled front gardens, represent the type of better-quality housing being built for the professional and white-collar workers that began to be constructed in the early 1890s. This was particularly the case on the western sides of British towns, as they faced the fresh, prevailing winds and

therefore had none of the industrial atmospheric pollution that was blown over to the eastern suburbs. In the background at the top of Wadham's Hill, poking through the trees as if to emphasise the theory, is the peculiar towered Victorian residence of the Kidson family, well-known wholesale grocers and provision merchants who were involved in local politics in the inter-war period. *D. R. Harvey collection*

Below The opening of the Arts & Industrial Exhibition at West Park by the Duke and Duchess of Connaught on 1 May 1902 was to be the town's equivalent of the Great Exhibition of 1851, and the tramcar service to the 'EXHIBITION' was inaugurated at the same time. Travelling along New Hampton Road East into

Wolverhampton town centre from West Park, or to be more exact Leicester Square, in the summer of 1902 is single-deck open-combination car 4, which had been in stock since the preceding January. The mother and her bonneted daughter watch the new tram go by as it passes the same terraces seen in the previous picture, between Dunkley Street and Drummond Street. Car 4 had been constructed by G. F. Milnes with two open ends and a short central saloon, with a seating layout of 8/16/8, and was mounted on Lorain-DuPont trucks. It was one of four combination cars in the original fleet of 12 trams and was withdrawn in 1921, although its trucks were reconditioned and used beneath new double-deck, top-covered tramcar 59. The original olive green

and gamboge livery of the first electric tramcars, with its highly varnished finish, suited the tramcar fleet extremely well and became the colours that were always used on the public service vehicles of Wolverhampton Corporation. *J. Hughes collection*

Above The large Higher Grade School stood on New Hampton Road East at the corner of Dunkley Street. Opened in 1894 at a cost of £14,500, it was given 'Secondary' status as a result of the 1902 Education Act, being extended to become the Municipal Secondary School in 1921, which name it still proclaims on the front frieze. It became the Municipal Grammar school from 1945 and subsequently part of the Colton Hill Comprehensive School, moving to new premises in Goldthorn Park in 1975. Today the old school

Newhampton Road, Wolverhampton. PUBLISHED BY C. SMITH

building is part of Wulfrun College. Travelling into the town centre is open-top, reverse-staircase, 48-seater double-deck car 6. Constructed by Milnes, it entered service in May 1902 and was mounted on Lorain-DuPont trucks, identifiable by their heavy external side bracing. The tram is carrying one of the typical local Edwardian tramcar advertisements, for the Wolverhampton Steam Laundry. Behind the tram, opposite the open space, which in later years was occupied by the West Park Infant School, is the prestigious three-storied Waterloo Terrace, built between 1852 and 1855. When built, the houses overlooked what in Victorian days was a racecourse, but there was some concern that the horse-racing fraternity and gambling was having a detrimental effect on the morals of the New Hampton Road East inhabitants! After the opening of the Dunstall Park racecourse, the former open space was re-landscaped and opened as West Park on Whit Monday 1881. *J. Hughes collection*

Above right Looking from Leicester Square along New Hampton Road East towards Waterloo Road in about 1923, a distant top-covered tram is making its way towards the town centre past the Municipal Secondary School using the newly installed overhead method. Leicester Square was

part of Whitmore Reans, which had been developed in the 1850s as a new suburb. 'Reans' is an old expression for drainage channels cut into poorly drained farmland, the word having the same derivation as the Somerset word 'rhyne', referring to drainage channels on the Somerset Levels, while Whitmore is thought to have been an earlier landlord in the area. Being over a mile from the town centre, the area soon had its own shops, church (St Andrew's, dating from 1865) and school (in Coleman Street, opened in 1860). The rarely used terminal stub-track to the left going into Coleman Street stands as a reminder that this was the Whitmore Reans terminus until 26 January 1905; despite the dirty, unused nature of the track, the line is still wired up for overhead operation. The No 2 tram route was re-opened with overhead current collection on 28 August 1921, although from Hunter Street terminus along New Hampton Road West to Tettenhall Road was not equipped for overhead operation. The land behind the three booted boys on the right, on the corner of Kingsland Road, is up for sale, having been in agricultural use until 1904! Kingsland Road, which was barely 100 yards long, led to the North Lodge and the conservatories in nearby West Park. *D. R. Harvey collection*

Left The tall young dandy on the left, with his pipe and straw boater, poses in the direction of the cameraman as he casually leans on his walking stick. Behind him, a young woman with ringlet-styled hair pushes a spindly-wheeled perambulator past the busy Whitmore Reans Post Office in Coleman Street in about 1905. The post box bears the crest of King Edward VII, which helps to date the view. On this warm summer's day, we are looking from the cut-back terminus in Coleman Street towards Leicester Square, with Jervis's tailor shop and an umbrella repair shop on the corner, where there is an empty open-topped tramcar. By the 1920s Jervis's shop had become a branch of Home & Colonial Stores and, not so surprisingly, the umbrella shop had ceased to trade, with a Mr F. C. Reed operating a barber's business from the premises. The distant car 24 was a reversed-staircase car fitted with Lorain-DuPont trucks, and was built by ER&TCW, entering service in October 1902. It is standing at the entrance of Kingsland Road and is facing the New Hampton Road West terminus. *D. R. Harvey collection*

Below left On every Victorian street corner throughout the country there always seemed to be a corner shop or a public house. The suburb of Whitmore Reans was no exception, although the shop on the corner of Coleman Street has developed into a row, the corner shop and the first seven premises being of a distinctly superior design to the remainder, distinguished by their double first-floor windows. Robert Melhuish's provisions store occupies the corner site, while next door round the corner is the West End Cafe. Car

16, another of the 13-18 class of G. F. Milnes double-deck trams, stands in the terminal stub in Coleman Street between 30 October 1903, when it was cut back from Newbridge, and its partial re-instatement along New Hampton Road West as far as Hunter Street on 26 January 1905. The tram is displaying the destination 'BILSTON RD', which was a financially unsuccessful cross-town service that ceased on 1 April 1905. The tram route was eventually abandoned on 1 October 1927, having been converted to the overhead electric collection method some six years earlier. *Bennett Clark*

Below The lychgate and decorative brick wall on the extreme right of New Hampton Road West belong to St Andrew's Church in Coleman Street, consecrated in 1865 and enlarged in 1892 to meet the religious requirements of the newly developed Whitmore Reans suburb. It was replaced in 1967 to the designs of Twentyman, Percy & Partners in a blocky, brick style. Just visible on the skyline is the other church in the area, the impressively towered Cranmore Wesleyan Chapel, which stood on the corner of Lloyd Street, within sight of Newbridge. A tiny little pony with a disproportionately large cart stands outside a shop that has its canvas canopy extended. These busy corner shops appear to be attracting a number of shoppers and passers-by. At the Hunter Street terminus of the Whitmore Reans tram route on the right, opposite Clifford Street, is tramcar 18. This tram is in its original condition, with an open top and unvestibuled platforms that became de rigueur after 1911 for the Wolverhampton tram fleet. This dates this autumn scene to between 1906 and 1910. *J. Hughes collection*

Below On a rainy day in January 1930, a motorbus turns into Court Road from New Hampton Road West. There is nothing unusual in this except that it is towards the end of the brief period when the 2 service was operated by motorbuses, the trams having been abandoned on 1 October 1927. The massive six-wheeled normal-control Guy CX is fitted with a 55-seater Dodson body; it has a drop chassis frame and a totally enclosed staircase. It had entered service in 1928 as 64 (UK 5364), and was renumbered 164 the following year. Above the bus are the trolleybus wires turning into Court Road for the electric buses that are about to be introduced, while standing on the corner opposite Wooldridge's grocery and provisions shop are three Corporation transport officials who are obviously 'checking out' something, as bus inspectors are born to do! Beyond the bus, New Hampton Road West can be seen dropping away towards Tettenhall Road and Newbridge. The block of bay-windowed houses on the right was among the last to be built in this road during the initial phase of its development, and date from the early years of the Edwardian period. *D. R. Harvey collection*

NEW HAMPTON ROAD, WOLVERHAMPTON.

Opposite bottom The section of track in New Hampton Road West beyond the Hunter Street terminus of the Whitmore Reans route was rarely used, despite the fact that it linked the end of the route to Tettenhall Road. After the Lorain Surface Contact system was converted to overhead on 28 August 1921 this section of track remained, but was not wired for overhead use. The reversing triangle at the bottom of New Hampton Road West at the junction with Tettenhall Road was, however, wired up, as it was the only place on the entire system where trams could be turned around. Here we are looking towards the spire of Cranmore Methodist Church from Tettenhall Road, which is barely 100 yards behind the photographer, and the tracks for the Lorain-powered trams lie unused. The terraced houses on both sides of the road were constructed at the very end of the 19th century; they had small walled front gardens and were larger than the earlier terraces around the Whitmore Reans tram terminus. The only traffic on the road is a pony and trap, while on the right a young girl stands with her hoop and stick watching the photographer with some curiosity. It is always sobering when looking at photographs of this age to wonder whatever became of the girl and what sort of life she led. *J. Hughes collection*

This page In 1909 the Red Cross Street Sunday School went on a trip to Tettenhall and hired three Corporation tramcars for the purpose. The pupils are waving Union Jack flags, but the infants on the tram in the top photograph seem to be less enthusiastic, possibly because of the presence of the large-hatted woman teacher on the top deck. The Red Cross Street School was one of only two elementary schools to be built by the Wolverhampton Education Board, while in the mid-1880s it became the home of the Corporation's first provision of nursery education in the town. The leading tram, carrying the infants, is car 18, which was the last of the six G. F. Milnes-bodied reverse-staircase trams, delivered in August 1902. The heavy framing of the Lorain-DuPont trucks looks somewhat antiquated when compared with the other trams in this convoy. The second tram, 35, carries on the balcony dash an

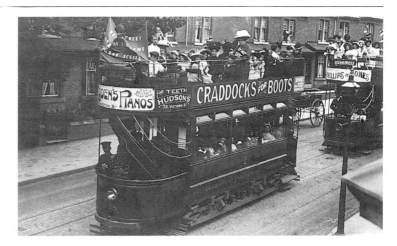

advertisement for Phillips & Jones's furniture store; it is a UEC 51-seater open-topper built in 1905 to the designs of the recently closed G. F. Milnes, but with direct staircases and mounted on a Brill 21E truck. This tram carries the girls, who seem marginally more cheerful than the senior boys occupying the third and last tramcar, which is of the same type as the girls' tram and is numbered 32. The three trams are posed in the section of New Hampton Road West beyond the normal Hunter Street terminus of the Whitmore Reans tram route. *D. R. Harvey collection*

Stafford Road services

The urban landscape along the line of the electric tram route to Stafford Road, Bushbury, has never followed the accepted pattern. The geographical convention is that the area just beyond the town centre should contain factories and a wide variety of industry, but in Wolverhampton's Stafford Road corridor that was not the case. At the start of the 20th century the best residences were in the Waterloo Road area near the post-1904 tram route, although the size and quality of the houses gradually deteriorated beyond the Red Roofs Hotel at Staveley Road. To the north, the 19th-century houses became meaner until the shops at Lower Stafford Street, Five Ways, were reached. This six-road junction was the hub of the local community, with a pub on every corner and in whose local houses many of the railway, gas and engineering workers lived.

The crossing of the road by the Great Western Railway, some 2 miles outside the town centre, led to the development of a heavy industrial zone. Stafford Road locomotive running shed was always an integral part of the large locomotive works, built by the Shrewsbury & Birmingham Railway in 1849 and inherited by the GWR. The works straddled Stafford Road, just beyond the magnificently low-arched skew brick bridge designed by the great man himself, Isambard Kingdom Brunel, and constructed locomotives as the only other GWR erecting shop outside Swindon until 1908, whereupon it became the North Division's main repair shop. Repair work continued until 11 February 1964, when the last steam locomotive, Churchward-designed 2-8-0 No 2859, left the works. Today the site is a light industrial estate.

Beyond the valley of Smestow Brook, which meanders through its valley to the north of Dunstall Hill from the Springfield area of Wolverhampton, and which attracted early Industrial Revolution water-powered slitting mills and small foundries, is the crossing of the Birmingham Canal at the junction with Jones Road. Dominating the skyline and the 'smell' of the area was the now long defunct Wolverhampton Gas Company works. The canal, for years characterised by the narrow bridge on Stafford Road, was the last piece of

James Brindley's jigsaw to be constructed as part of his 'Golden Cross' scheme. This section of the canal went from the centre of Wolverhampton at the Can Lane Basin to the Staffs & Worcester Canal at Aldersley Junction, and was finally opened on 21 September 1772, just eight days before Brindley's death. To the north-east of the canal was a site that developed into one of Wolverhampton's largest manufacturers. The Electric Construction Company built a huge factory in a 23-acre triangular site nestling beneath Oxley Bank between Stafford Road and Bushbury Lane, which opened in 1890. The company produced heavy electrical machinery, electric motors and generating equipment and eventually employed about 1,500 workers. It closed in 1985 and was again replaced by a series of light industrial initiatives, called the Wolverhampton Science Park, which spilled over on to the former gasworks site. Nearby, at the junction with Bushbury Lane, is Strykers, a huge ten-pin-bowling complex located behind the Island House, which was formerly the Croft public house, standing between Gorsebrook Road and Bushbury Lane. This pub was in sight of where the trams reached their terminus at the edge of the then Edwardian Wolverhampton and, strangely, adjacent to both large industrial premises and countryside.

The Stafford Road tram service was developed almost as an extension of Wolverhampton Wanderers' Molineux football ground siding, running to the north of the town centre. The quality of the housing once Darlington Street was left behind was immediately of a higher standard once the trams turned right into Waterloo Road South. The original electric tram route as far as Bushbury Lane along Stafford Road was an extension of the Molineux football ground siding off the Whitmore Reans route, and was included in the new route to Bushbury Lane, which opened on 13 August 1904 and left the town along the western side of the Wolverhampton Wanderers ground in Waterloo Road North. The town terminus was in Victoria Square and the trams processed out to the football ground by way of Lichfield Street and Darlington Street. By 1915, the arrangements for the football match siding alongside the wall of the football ground had been modified since the original opening in 1902, with the single running track being connected to the siding at both ends and the siding being moved so that kerbside loading was available for football supporters. The 3 route, numbered as such in 1915, was only operational using the overhead system between 1 October 1921 and August 1924, after the conversion of the trams from the Lorain system; the state of the tram tracks was sufficiently poor to prompt abandonment, and the trams finally ceased to run on 19 August 1924. However, the still fairly new electrical supply infrastructure made this, and all Wolverhampton's tram routes, prime candidates for replacement by 'trackless' trams, and trolleybuses consequently replaced the temporary bus service on 9 March 1925 as far as Bushbury Lane, making it the second such route to be operated by this mode of transport.

The new single-deck trolleybuses, unlike the trams, left the town by way of Wulfruna Street and Molineux Street and back via an anti-clockwise loop by way of North Street, passing the Town Hall, and into Queen Square. On turning into Molineux Street, the trolleybuses passed the Wolves ground on the other side of the ground to the equivalent tram route. On reaching the Red Roofs Hotel, the trolleybuses turned into Waterloo Road and followed the tram route to Bushbury Lane and now beyond to Fordhouses. The inbound trolleybuses eventually followed Wulfruna Street, passing the rear of St Peter's Collegiate Church and into the northern half of Princes Square, when the route to Bushbury Hill was opened on 31 November 1931. In addition, the section of road between Stafford Street, at its junction with Cannock Road and Lower Stafford Street, towards Five Ways was wired up in order to allow the movement of trolleybuses into the town centre by way of Stafford Road without getting caught up in the Saturday crowds going to and from home football games at Molineux.

Beyond the old tram terminus, the trolleybus route was extended up Oxley Bank and on through what was initially virtually open countryside, to a new terminus at The Vine country public house with its cluster of houses at Wobaston Road, Fordhouses. This began operation on 23 April 1925. On Stafford Road, the mixture of Boer War-vintage houses mixed with the early 1920s municipal housing on

Oxley Bank gave way to the huge Goodyear Tyre factory, opened in 1927, thereby fitting into the contemporary urban landscape. At its peak, by the mid-1960s, the Goodyear factory was employing more than 5,000 people. Beyond the factory, the housing included an impressive series of privately owned bungalows on both sides of the road, those on the east backing on to Wingfoot Park, one of the few parks on the north side of Wolverhampton, before reaching the next major road junction at Marsh Lane, which in post-war years would give access to the Wobaston Estate. Another clutch of shops and the impressive Three Tuns public house, built in 1930, guard this junction., which also saw one of Stafford Road's first sections of dual carriageway.

Post-war developments gradually began to nibble away at the green belt, although there was ribbon development along Stafford Road, and it was this that was served by the number 3 trolleybus route. In Wolverhampton, despite the fact that by about 1930 the trolleybus system had become 'the largest in the world', the days of expansion were quite brief, so that once the major arterial roads and any other services provided by the trams had been converted, only a brief period of expansion occurred; by 1935, when the Penn Road extension was opened, any new services were developed by motorbuses. Once away from the Stafford Road trolleybus route, most of the other motorbus services were not developed until after the Second World War. However, the earliest, using Bushbury Lane, was perhaps the most important, this being the Low Hill service via the town and Fighting Cocks as far as Twelfth Avenue, opened on 5 December 1927. The Bushbury/Low Hill area was emerging as an extremely large housing development and a further new motorbus service, this time using double-deckers, was inaugurated on 10 July 1934; this was the 33 service, which passed Bushbury Church. In the late 1940s the new estate of Northwood Park was served by the clockwise 41 route via Wood Lane, beginning on 13 June 1949, while the extended 33 became the anti-clockwise service in Northwood Park. The Rake Gate Estate off Oxley Moor Road was developed on land that had formerly belonged to Rakegate Farm, and was served by the 44 bus route, introduced on 27 November 1950, while the 28 service to Patshull Avenue, Wobaston, was opened on 9 April 1951; this not only served the housing estate but also the industrial complexes on the north side of Wobaston Road.

The trolleybus service to The Vine, Fordhouses, was abandoned on 26 January 1964, when its 'other half' to Bushbury Hill via Cannock Road was closed. Beyond the Fordhouses Estate at the trolleybus terminus, a number of large industrial premises were built including, on the edge of the old Pendeford aerodrome, the Boulton Paul aircraft factory, famous for its briefly successful 'Defiant' Rolls-Royce Merlin-powered two-seater night-fighter of the Second World War; today the company survives today as Dowty Aerospace. Nearby, H. M. Hobson, a precision engineering company, moved to a new pre-war 'shadow factory' situated on Stafford Road, which in the 1950s

saw a massive increase in its workforce; it was later taken over in 1970 by Lucas Aerospace.

Routes beyond Fordhouses were obviously operated by motorbuses, and the 22 service to the large village of Brewood was first operated as a regular service on 16 August 1922, after objections to running buses over country lanes by a number of Rural District Councils. The former Midland Red service to Wheaton Aston, inaugurated in March 1922, did not use Stafford Road, going instead by way of Albrighton, but when operated by the Corporation, after 12 August 1929, the village was served by an extension of the Brewood service by way of the villages of Stretton and Lapley. These country bus routes were inherited by the PTE, but were transferred to Midland Red in September 1973.

Motorbus services in the town centre

Below Between mid-1931 and the autumn of 1934, Wolverhampton Corporation did not purchase any motorbuses. This contrasted greatly with the situation with the trolleybus fleet, for which there were 51 additions of increasingly up-to-date Sunbeam and Guy chassis. If the policy to support local trolleybus chassis builders was pursued with vigour, because they were probably as good as the anything in production elsewhere, then the same could not be said of the bus side of the equation. The Guy 'Arab', introduced in 1933 as a successor to the 'Invincible' and 'Conquest' models, was the first double- or single-deck chassis to be built in the country that offered only a diesel, or, as they were called at the time, oil engine. The Gardner

5LW and 6LW engines were quickly developing an excellent reputation for reliability and economy, but the chassis were generally only available with four-speed crash transmissions. The management at Guy Motors must have sat with bated breath for the large orders to come in for their new model, not least from Mr Silver's office in Cleveland Road. As the waiting at Park Lane began to get a little worrying, at the 1933 Olympia Commercial Motor Show Daimler introduced the COG5, a chassis that in many ways was similar to the slightly heavier 'Arab', but which offered the Wilson fluid coupling and pre-selective epicyclic gearbox. At a stroke the Guy was relegated to the category of Morris-Commercial, TSM and Thornycroft. Even the local

Wolverhampton Corporation was not impressed, purchased just two single-deckers and one double-decker! By way of contrast, after buying two Daimler COG5 single-deckers in 1934, this model quickly became the standard for the Corporation. The COG5 seen here, 304 (JW 8104), with the standard style of Brush body, was built in 1936, and about 12 years later is working on the 33 service to Bushbury Church, waiting in Wulfruna Street alongside the Wolverhampton & Staffordshire Technical College. The photograph shows that the mid-1930s pre-war bus fleet did not fare very well in the survival stakes, and many of them, including 304, with composite Brush Engineering bodies, showed distinct signs of body sag. It was withdrawn in 1950. *D. R. Harvey collection*

Above right The 44 service to the Rake Gate Estate was introduced on 27 November 1950. It started in Wulfruna Street and, having turned into Stafford Street, entered Stafford Road at Five Ways. The route continued to follow the trolleybus wires as far as Oxley Moor Road, where it turned left, then right into the Rake Gate Estate, terminating at Sheldon Road. The site of this post-war housing estate was still open countryside near the Shropshire Union Canal until the beginning of 1948, yet the first council semi-detached houses were occupied by the beginning of 1949. 519 (FJW 519), a Brush-bodied Daimler CVG6 that entered service in February 1950, was still fairly new when it was photographed in Wulfruna Street, next to the College's early post-war extension. It must be close to leaving time, for although the driver, in his summer dust-jacket, and his conductress are talking to another member of the bus staff as

the bus loads, another member of the public is running to catch the 44 service. *W. J. Haynes*

Below Swinging around the island in Princes Square as it turns into Wulfruna Street from Stafford Street is Park Royal-bodied Guy 'Arab' V 133 (133 DDA). To the right of the bus, which appears to be showing the wrong destination display, is The Vine Hotel, owned by the local Butlers Brewery. Behind the Minivan and the four-door Ford Corsair 120E saloon in Stafford Street is the TA Drill Hall and the Registry Office. Sneaking up the nearside of the bus is a Bedford CA Mark II van. The bus is working on the 33 service from Bushbury in October 1965, during the period when the two Bushbury services, 33 and 41, were briefly altered to terminate in Exchange Street, which runs between Wulfruna Street and Queen Square. This situation was not popular and both routes quickly reverted to Wulfruna Street only two months later. *A. D. Broughall*

Above Coming in the opposite direction out of Wulfruna Street and into Stafford Street, with The George Hotel in the background, is 183 (HJW 183D). Today this pub is the Varsity Tavern, while in the background at the far end of Wulfruna Street is the remains of the old Market Hall. The bus is one of the rare AEC 'Renowns', which were the only ones bodied by Weymann to the specification of Nottingham City Transport other than those supplied direct to that East Midlands city. Nottingham's 42 'Renown' chassis were to the 3B3RA specification, which meant that they had four-speed synchromesh gearboxes, whereas the Wolverhampton ones had monocontrol four-speed direct selection epicyclic gearboxes (ie 'twiddlers'). The bus is working on the 41 service, and although it is still in the municipal green and yellow colours, it has the Fablon-stickers indicating its new West Midlands PTE owners. All of Wolverhampton's five 'Renowns' were repainted into WMPTE blue and cream livery, and 183 lasted until 1975. *A. J. Douglas*

Left On a wet day in Wulfruna Street, looking towards Princes Square from the side of St Peter's Gardens, is a Daimler CVG6 with a well-muffed radiator. Brush-bodied 504 (FJW 504) dates from 1948 and is loading up with somewhat wet-looking passengers. It is working on the 33 service, and displays the destination 'WENTWORTH ROAD VIA BUSHBURY LANE'. It was not long since the route had been operated by hired coaches, a situation that applied from November 1947 until mid-July 1949, caused by the shortage of buses and the opening of a number of new services in the early post-war period. The 33 service had been opened through the developing Low Hill Estate to Bushbury Church as early as 10 July 1934, and although it perhaps was not appreciated at the time, it really marked the end of the expansion of the all-powerful trolleybus 'empire', for no new trolleybus routes were built after that year, only extensions of existing ones. *M. Rooum*

Top Between 1935 and 1938 Wolverhampton purchased 48 double-decker Daimler COG5s, all of which had Brush bodywork. This combination was also found in the Midlands area at the municipalities of Coventry and Derby, and the similarities in the body-style of the Brush bodies supplied to all three were considerable. Waiting at the rear of St Peter's Church, with the rear of the School of Art building looking down over Wulfruna Street in about 1948, is bus 349 (BJW 149). This 55-seater bus had entered service in April 1938 and would be the only one of the batch of 12 to be taken out of service in 1952. The lower saloon offside destination boxes had not been used in the post-war years. 349 is well loaded with passengers for the journey to Bushbury Church, but is still awaiting its driver. *D. R. Harvey collection*

Middle Waiting to depart from the same spot in Wulfruna Street at the end of St Peter's Close, but now in the mid-1950s, is one of the first post-war buses supplied to the undertaking. There is by now a concrete bus shelter alongside the wall of the gardens of St Peter's Church, next to which is 387 (FJW 387), a Guy 'Arab' III with a Brush H29/25R body. This bus entered service in 1949 and is working on the 28 service to the post-war Wobaston Estate, which had been developed to the north-west of Stafford Road near The Three Tuns public house. Behind it is 362 (DJW 762), a wartime Guy 'Arab' II chassis with a Gardner 5LW engine dating from 1943. The higher radiator of the Mark II 'Arab' can be appreciated when compared to the later post-war 'Arab' III's low-mounted radiator. 362 was rebodied by Roe with a H31/25R body in 1952, and is standing waiting for its driver before going to Blakeley Green on the 34 route. *C. W. Routh*

Bottom The 98 service to Old Fallings Lane, Bushbury Hill, usually started in Cleveland Street and went through the town centre before duplicating the former Bushbury Hill trolleybus service, which had been replaced by motorbuses in January 1964. The 3 route was split in October 1965 and the 98 motorbus service became the northern leg, with the Fordhouses route along Stafford Road retaining its original number.

Loaded with passengers, but sans chauffeur, is Guy 'Arab' V 96 (7096 UK), with a Weymann-built body manufactured in Addlestone, Surrey, to the standard MCW 'Orion' pattern. It is parked in Whitmore Street, just off Stafford Street, where only a few years earlier the Jeffcock Road trolleybuses had their town terminus. On the right is what in later years became the infamous Lafayette Night Club, but which in 1967 was an ordinary cafe. *R. H. G. Simpson*

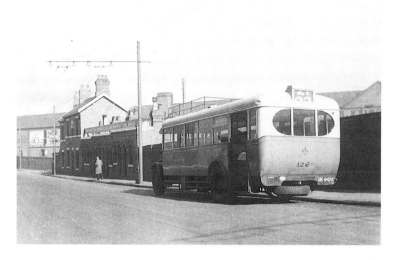

Top Facing the wrong way in Railway Street alongside the wall of the Birmingham Canal Basin is the ultimate example of the 1920s Wolverhampton single-decker fleet. Petrol-engined Guy 'Conquest' FC 78 (UK 6478), a Guy-bodied 35-seater that entered service in 1929, stands facing the huge warehouse alongside the Birmingham Canal at the Shropshire Union Wharf. It is after 1934, as by that date the bus had been renumbered 178. However, it did not seem to make much difference to its life-span, as it would be withdrawn in 1938 as a vehicle deemed obsolete. Just beyond the bus are the buildings of Can Lane Wharf, which advertises itself 'for coal and bricks'. The bus is working on the 22 service to the village of Brewood, beyond Coven Heath on Stafford Road. *D. R. Harvey collection*

Middle By the early post-war years, the Stafford Road services, including that to Brewood, parked in Railway Street, alongside Can Lane Wharf facing Victoria Square before turning into Railway Drive, which faced the High Level Station. Standing empty in about 1948 is austere-looking Guy 'Arab' II 369 (DJW 769), one of three Strachan-bodied buses allocated to Wolverhampton by the Ministry of War Transport in 1944. Strachan bodies were fairly unusual in the West Midlands where Weymann, Park Royal, Brush and Duple examples were more usually found. 369 is still carrying its original, uncompromisingly square-looking 56-seater body, which will be replaced with a comparatively curvaceous Charles Roe body in 1951. The bus is working on the 22 service to Brewood, which must have been hard work for the driver, especially along the country lanes near that village, with its heavy steering, underpowered Gardner 5LW 7-litre diesel engine and 'back-to-front' gearbox. *S. N. J. White*

Bottom Loading up with passengers prior to leaving on the 22 service to Brewood is an impressive six-wheeled double-decker. The little girl holding her mother's hand on the extreme right walks towards the imposing-looking double-decker and has the prospect of climbing two very steep steps just to gain access to the rear platform. 58 (UK 5258) is a forward-control Guy CX with a Dodson H30/25R body that entered service in 1928, and is seen in Queen Square beneath the equestrian statue of Prince Albert, who looks benignly down on the intending passengers some five years later, for in 1934 the bus was renumbered 158. The bus is adorned with advertisements for the local Butler's Ales, Preedy's tobacco, and the strange advertisement for Typhoo Tea that proclaims it as an aid for indigestion, although the wording might be construed that the tea actually encourages that ailment! 58 survived in service until 1938, together with 11 other Guy CXs, being replaced by a dozen Daimler COG5s with Brush bodywork that were delivered during the same year. The style of the bodywork is redolent of tramcars, with an almost clerestory arrangement for the lower saloon windows; this added to the vintage appearance of these buses, which were the mainstay of the Wolverhampton motorbus fleet from around 1926 until 1929, when some 26 similar vehicles were purchased from Guy Motors. *W. J. Haynes*

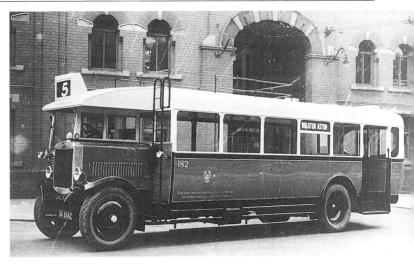

Above right Although parked in Cleveland Road outside the Corporation's main depot, this was the type of single-decker bus used on the 'country services' to villages such as Brewood and Wheaton Aston at the turn of the 1930s. 82 (UK 6582), a Guy-bodied Guy FC, is adorned with a roof ladder that gives access to the rather rudimentary luggage rack mounted on the front half of the roof. The ladder and rack were unusual fittings for a single-decker of this vintage, but somehow represented the use of this and similar buses during the 1930s. This 35-seater characterised the typical Corporation single-decker of the period and was in fact the last of six FCs delivered to the undertaking between 1928 and 1929. *D. R. Harvey collection*

Trolleybuses to Fordhouses

A pair of pre-war trolleybuses wait at the loading stands in Wulfruna Street outside the Wolverhampton & Staffordshire Technical College in about 1947, which by this time had been established for nearly 20 years. The leading trolleybus, working on the 3 service to Bushbury Hill having come into town from Fordhouses, is 243 (JW 8143). This Sunbeam MF2 entered service on 27 March 1937 and belonged to the first generation of four-wheeled double-deck trolleybuses bought by the undertaking. The change in policy from six-wheelers to four-wheelers took place in 1935, and 243 was one of a batch of six Park Royal-bodied MF2s. The model had been introduced in January 1934, and JW 8143 was the 50th chassis to be constructed. However, as far as the British market is concerned this gives a somewhat false picture of the scale of Sunbeam's output; of the first 50 MFs, export orders accounted for double-deckers for Durban and Johannesburg in South Africa and a batch of 15 MF3A single-deckers for Rangoon in Burma. In all, 120 MF-type four-wheelers were produced by Sunbeam at its Moorfield Road factory in Blakenhall, and Wolverhampton Corporation, supporting local industry in the Depression of

the 1930s, bought 45 of them! Behind 243 is 295 (DDA 995) working on the 9A service to Bushbury Hill; this was the last of all the pre-war Sunbeam MF2s to be built. Delivered from Charles Roe in full fleet livery, it entered service on 4 April 1942, only ten months before the first wartime-specification W4 model entered service. *W. J. Haynes*

Above About 15 years later, waiting at the same shelters in Wulfruna Street, motorbuses had begun to make an impact on the trolleybus scene. Bus 6 (SUK 6), a Meadows-engined Guy 'Arab' IV with an 'Orion'-style Metro-Cammell H33/27R body, had entered service in March 1957 and is working on the 41 service. This bus route, developed in the early post-war years, followed the Fordhouses trolleybus service along Stafford Road, turning off into Bushbury Lane near Dunstall Park racecourse, then into Fordhouse Road, Bushbury, before terminating in the Northwood Park Estate.

The bus is overtaking the two parked trolleybuses outside the Wulfruna Street extension of the original 1926 Technical College, built to the designs of Col Lowbridge, the architect to the County Education Department, and opened on 30 June 1933 by Marquess Dufferin. The trolleybus carrying the advertisement for Sunfresh orange squash and working on the 3 route to Bushbury Hill is Roe-rebodied Sunbeam W4 434 (EJW 434), while behind it is an unidentified Park Royal-rebodied trolleybus with the same type of chassis, also going to Bushbury Hill. *J. C. Brown*

Left The Wolverhampton bus and trolleybus fleet looked its best in the early 1950s when the vehicles were still reasonably new and body maintenance and livery condition were regarded as a matter of municipal pride. Standing in Wulfruna Street, facing Princes Square, are examples of both types of post-war trolleybus bought by the undertaking, albeit with the same design of 8-foot-wide Park Royal body. Opposite is the rear of the Art Gallery, which at this time would have been used as the Art College, with the ornamental gardens of St Peter's Collegiate Church, laid out in 1936, in the background. The leading trolleybus, on the Bushbury Hill 3 service, is Guy BT 640 (FJW 640), which has come into town from

Fordhouses up the hill from North Street and the distant Market Place. It is carrying a curiously Birmingham-based set of advertisements; above the destination boxes is one for Barbers coffee essence, from the firm located in Ladywell Walk near the Birmingham Hippodrome, and along the side one for Atkinson's Ales of Aston. Parked behind 640, also working on the 3 service, is Sunbeam F4 465 (FJW 465). Between them is an unidentified Brush-bodied motorbus on the 41 route to Northwood Park Estate, which will travel northwards out of town by way of Stafford Road. *R. Hannay*

Right The back rooms of the Art Gallery were used as the Art College until 1972, when the new College of Art and Design was opened on St Peter's Ring Road. Parked outside this building in Wulfruna Street facing Molineux Street, at the primitive corrugated-iron-roofed shelters, is pre-war trolleybus 284 (DDA 184). This Sunbeam MF2 with a Roe H29/25R body had that bodybuilder's patent staircase employing two right-angle turns on the way to and from the upper saloon. An intending passenger runs to catch his bus, which is waiting to go to Fordhouses on the 3 route and carries above its damaged lower panels an advertisement for Keiller's Dundee Marmalade, which contained lovely large chunks of orange peel! The trolleybus entered service on 10 June 1940 but only lasted until the final day of November 1950 when it was withdrawn, eventually turning up as a caravan in Bilbrook. *R. Marshall*

Below Although a few properties have been demolished and those ghastly shelters have also gone, Wulfuna Street remains largely unaltered on 26 March 1963. Quietly humming away at the stop is trolleybus 403 (DJW 903), a wartime Sunbeam W4 with a 1952 Park Royal body, working on the 3 route to Fordhouses, and facing North Street. Behind, parked outside the Candy Stores, are an Austin A40 Devon, a Ford Anglia 105E, an Austin A35 van, a Triumph Herald and a Ford Thames 307E van, which was based on the Anglia car. The five-storey building on the left occupying the corner site of Princes Square is the Royal London Mutual Assurance premises, which opened in 1902. *P. J. Thompson*

Top After the introduction of the route to Fordhouses on 9 March 1925, the trolleybuses briefly ran into town on an anti-clockwise loop around North Street, Queen Square, Lichfield Street and Wulfruna Street. This appears to have ceased after the trams were replaced on the Wolverhampton Wanderers football specials at the end of the 1925 season. Single-decker Tilling-Stevens TS6 trolleybus 10 (DA 9010) is about to travel into North Street on its inward journey into town from Fordhouses; on the left are the outbound wires from Wulfruna Street. Across the Market Place, where a market had been held since the Royal Charter of 1258, is the symmetrically styled Market Hall. The trolleybus has just passed, on the corner of North Street on the extreme right, a shop that made, re-covered and repaired umbrellas. In the distance can just be made out the Old Mitre public house and Jessops Hotel, which stood next to each other. The Civic Hall, opened in 1938, replaced these buildings. *D. R. Harvey collection*

Middle Standing at the bus stop outside the old market buildings in about 1936 is a single-deck trolleybus working on the 3A route to Fordhouses. 211 (JW 4311), a 1934 Guy BT with a Park Royal B32R body and in the pre-war livery, which included a primrose-painted roof, is being overtaken in Wulfruna Street by a cyclist. This trolleybus was bought for use on the low-bridge trolleybus services, including those to Wednesfield and Fordhouses. After the road beneath Wednesfield Road bridge was lowered in the latter part of 1943, the need for single-deckers was removed, resulting in their withdrawal, many as early as 1945; 211 was withdrawn after an accident on 31 January 1944. This pre-war view suggests that this late flowering of the single-deckers, four Guy BTs and seven Sunbeam MF1s, left them somewhat underused, hence their use on other rush-hour service extras. *D. R. Harvey collection*

Bottom Travelling along North Street in about 1925, with the Market Hall and Cheapside behind the photographer, is trolleybus 10 (DA 9010), a Tilling-Stevens TS6 with a Dodson B36C body that had entered service on 28 February 1925. The solid-tyred trolleybus succumbed to old age in 1937, but its after-life was perhaps more interesting than its somewhat prosaic service life.

Birmingham industrialist Mr Martin of Handsworth Wood bought it on 13 May 1937 and had it transported by the GWR to Bow Street Station near Aberystwyth, whereupon it was towed to a field near Clarach Bay, surviving as his holiday home until 1966!. Seven trolleybuses (8-14) were ordered for the Bushbury tram conversion, and the 'twin-wire' service was immediately extended along Stafford Road to a new terminus at Wobaston Road, Fordhouses, on 9 March 1925, becoming the Corporation's second trolleybus conversion from trams. The Bushbury tram route came into the town by way of Waterloo Road and Darlington Street, but when the trolleybuses were introduced they avoided this junction and came into town by way of North Street and Queen Square, and out via Wulfruna Street and Molineux Street, regaining Waterloo Road at the junction with Dunkley Street and Staveley Road. The trolleybus is in front of Wolverhampton's impressive 1871 Town Hall, designed by E. Bates in a vaguely French chateau style. *D. R. Harvey collection*

Top right One of the motorbus services that passed along Stafford Road was the 28 route, introduced on 9 April 1951 in order to serve the early post-war Wobaston housing estate. It followed the trolleybuses along Stafford Road as far as The Three Tuns public house, before turning left into Marsh Lane and right into Patshull Avenue before arriving at its terminus at Wobaston Road, about 200 yards from the Fordhouses trolleybus terminus. Loading up with passengers in front of the old Market Hall site, with Cheapside running at right angles off North Street and the Town Hall to

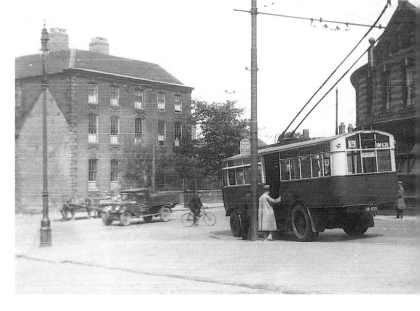

the right, is one of the trolleybus replacement buses that was delivered in November 1963. Guy 'Arab' V 84 (7084 UK) is a Weymann forward-entrance 72-seater bus powered by a Gardner 6LW 8.4-litre engine. The previous 50 double-deckers had been full-fronted Guy 'Arab' IVs, which looked modern but had the disadvantage of having an inaccessible engine, so all future double-deckers reverted to the half-cab layout with a Birmingham-style concealed radiator. By this time the old Market Hall site was being employed as a car park, with a Vauxhall Victor FC being prominent. In Cheapside, behind the bus, is the Imperial Garden, one of the earliest Chinese restaurants in the town. *R. H. G. Simpson*

Above right Picking up its passengers in Wulfruna Street in about 1928, outside The Chequer Ball public house, is one of Wolverhampton's first generation of trolleybuses, which had entered service on 11 November 1926. This one is single-decker 26 (UK 626), a Tilling-Stevens TS6 with a Dodson 36-seater centre-entrance body, which by this time was running

on pneumatic tyres. The trolleybus is working on the 3A route to Fordhouses, which despite its suffix letter was the original trolleybus terminus. If a vehicle was showing just the destination number 3, it would be going only just beyond the old tram terminus at Bushbury Lane to a turning circle at Oxley Moor Road, Oxley. Behind the Ford A 15cwt light lorry speeding into North Street is the lovely Giffard House. This dates from 1728 and is characteristically an Early Georgian brick-built town house with two and a half storeys and five bays. It was built by a Francis Smith of Warwick for Peter Giffard of Chillington, a well-known local Roman Catholic activist, who handed the house over to the local Roman Catholic authorities in 1734. Hidden within what looked like a prosperous merchant's house was a chapel in which the local Catholics could worship at a time when Catholicism was a dangerous religion to be following. In 1989 the building was lovingly restored together with the church of St Peter and St Paul of 1826, but in 1928 it was looking considerably down at heel. *D. R. Harvey collection*

Above Having turned from Wulfruna Street in front of the decorated brickwork on the rounded corner of The Chequer Ball public house, trolleybus 441 (EJW 441), a 1947 Sunbeam W4 rebodied by Charles Roe in June 1960, is standing at the bus stop just beyond the Belisha crossing in North Street. Just visible on the extreme left is Giffard House and the Roman Catholic Presbytery, while in front of the trolleybus is Wadham's Hill, a road that today has been completely lost under the Ring Road. Beyond the Fordhouses-bound 441 is the Molineux Hotel. This wonderful three-storey Georgian town house was built in the late 1740s for Benjamin Molineux, whose family were wealthy ironmongers and merchants. This three-storey building with additional wings became a hotel in 1870 after having been bought by O. E. McGregor in 1860. The grounds behind the house became pleasure gardens and were used for sporting events, the most popular being cycle races. It was here that Wolverhampton Wanderers played their first games, having turned professional in 1888 and becoming one of the 12 founder-members of the Football League. Behind the hotel the club built its new football ground, which today is the famous Molineux Stadium. Piercing the sky is one of the floodlight pylons that served to illuminate the Wolves' home. The Molineux ground was first equipped with floodlights in 1953, although these lights, almost 150 feet tall, are on one of four pylons erected in 1957. While the football ground has been transformed by the investments of the Hayward family since 1991, the old hotel, separated from the town by the Ring Road, now lies derelict, having closed in 1979. Sadly, Wolves failed again to get into the Premiership in May 2002, casting more 'doom and gloom' over this part of the city. *J. C. Brown*

Opposite above The last bus stop coming into town from Fordhouses was in North Street opposite Wadham's Hill.

Discharging its passengers outside Woodall's shoe repair shop is 466 (FJW 466), before it travels around the corner at The Chequer Ball and into Wulfruna Street, which was the main pick-up point in the town centre for the 3 route. Woodall's Shoe Service shop has a sign for locally produced Goodyear soles and heels in its window, a far cry from the tyres for which the Wolverhampton-based company is better known. The trolleybus is a Sunbeam F4 with a Park Royal 8-foot-wide 54-seater body that entered service on 20 October 1948 and would survive until 31 July 1965, when it failed by just one week to see out the trolleybus services to Bilston, Darlaston and Whitmore Reans. Working on the 3 route and travelling to Bushbury Hill via Park Lane, it is still fitted with the trolleybase shrouds on the roof in this October 1959 view, which would be removed from nearly all the FJW-registered trolleybuses in the next two years. *D. F. Parker*

Right The Molineux football ground was first used by Wolverhampton Wanderers on 2 September 1889, and the first time it was served by public transport was by the Lorain tram system. The siding for football matches was opened as a branch northwards from the existing Whitmore Reans tram route on 20 September 1902 and ran along the side of the ground on Waterloo Road. On 13 October 1904 the tram route along Stafford Road as far as Bushbury was opened in order to serve the works traffic of both the Great Western Railway and the London & North Western Railway at their respective locomotive depots, as well as the huge Electric Construction Company's factory at Showell Road. The new track is nearing completion in this summer 1902 view, with workmen welding and preparing the central strip for the surface contact studs that would power the trams. Beyond the distant cable drum can just be made out the Red Roofs Hotel at the apex of Staveley Road and Waterloo Road. *J. Hughes collection*

Above Although the abandonment of the trams to Bushbury took place on 19 August 1924, it was not until St George's Day the following year that the replacement trolleybus service was able to become operational. Meanwhile the football match traffic was still served by the trams, which reverted to their 1902 modus operandi with the Waterloo Road tracks reverting to being little more than a siding. This lasted until the end of the soccer season on 2 May 1925, when all the football traffic was handled by buses and trolleybuses. On 9 March 1925 the new trolleybus service to Fordhouses was instigated, but unlike the tramcar service, which, through a quirk of the route's development, had been linked into the Whitmore Reans service, this ran out of town by way of North Street and down the other side of the Molineux Ground. On Monday 30 December 1963 two trolleybuses, 447 (EJW 447) and 442 (EJW 442), both Roe-rebodied Sunbeam W4s, stand alongside the corrugated steel wall of the football ground's eastern stand in Molineux Street opposite Vincent Street. At the bottom of the hill, with Waterloo Road crossing from left to right, is the Red Roofs Hotel, serving once again as an excellent geographical marker. *J. C. Brown*

Opposite above Double-decker tram 3 was built by the ER&TCW and entered service in May 1902, mounted on Brill 21E trucks and originally fitted with reverse staircases; it was fitted with enclosed platforms in the years before the Great War, but was never top covered. Despite this lack of upper saloon protection, the tram was converted to overhead operation from the original Lorain Surface Contact system.

The Bushbury tram route was converted to overhead power supply on 1 October 1921, making it the sixth of the eight tram routes to be modified. Tram 3 is in Waterloo Road having descended the hill from the nearby Molineux football ground, and will take the slight curve to the right into Waterloo Road North, with its large Victorian villas and long narrow back gardens. Beyond the tram, on the corner of Staveley Road, is the Red Roofs Hotel, which today is called The Goal Post. *D. R. Harvey collection*

Right Looking back towards the town, on a sunny, summer's day in 1961, Roe-rebodied Sunbeam W4 419 (DUK 419) comes out of Molineux Street into Waterloo Road; having just passed in front of it is a Morris Mini Minor. The former tram route up the hill of Waterloo Road was abandoned in 1924; a section of wiring was put up in 1941 towards the Molineux football ground, but was subsequently never used for normal services. Presumably with the deteriorating situation in the Second World War after the evacuation of the BEF at Dunkirk, the Corporation was looking for another way out of the town centre for the trolleybuses in the event of aerial bombardment at the level that had been suffered by the cities of Coventry and Birmingham in November 1940. Parked beyond the crossroads sign is a Surrey-registered Hillman Minx Phase I of March 1946, which when new had cost £474 plus Purchase Tax. On the corner of Dunkley Street and Staveley Road is Crow's newsagent and tobacconist shop, while the wall on the extreme right belongs to the Red Roofs Hotel. *J. C. Brown*

Above Coming out of town along Waterloo Road on 30 December 1963 and working on the 3 route to Fordhouses is trolleybus 443 (FJW 443), another of the Sunbeam W4 chassis of 1947, which re-entered service on 7 February 1962 with a new 7ton 13cwt Charles Roe body that increased its previous carrying capacity by six, making it a 60-seater. 443 looks in need of a repaint, and five months later it would emerge from Cleveland Road garage paintshop in pristine condition, albeit for the last time. It is almost at the junction with Francis Street where there was a workmen's boarding house run 'strictly and efficiently' by Miss Mary Lewis. In the foreground on the left is the junction with Oxley Street. The houses along this stretch of the route, immediately before the Five Ways junction, dated from the 1850-80s and were far less grand than the terraces and villas nearer town beyond the distant Red Roofs Hotel. This rather reflected the area's proximity to the large industrial complexes that the trolleybus is approaching. *J. C. Brown*

Opposite above Leaning over as it swings around the traffic island at Five Ways on its way into Wolverhampton is Sunbeam F4 trolleybus 470 (FJW 470). This fully loaded Park Royal-bodied trolleybus entered service on 23 October 1948 and is about to pass into Waterloo Road from Stafford Road on 16 July 1962. In front of it, hidden by the mock-half-timbered public toilets, is the Wellington public house, which for many years was an Atkinson's hostelry, standing at the junction of North Road and Waterloo Road. Hidden by the trolleybus is the appropriately named Locomotive Inn, while to the left is one of the many newsagents and tobacconists in

the area. The photograph was taken in Lower Stafford Street, which was wired for trolleybuses coming in and out of town, so that they could avoid the football traffic in Molineux Street on match days. *J. C. Brown*

Right The view just after the Great War from Five Ways towards Brunel's magnificent 'skew bridge', which took the Great Western Railway over Stafford Road, shows a typical industrial suburb that could almost be anywhere, except for the total lack of tram overhead. Next door to the drapery shop on the left is the Locomotive Inn, one of many in the area that slaked the thirsts of Black Country railwaymen, particularly on a Friday night after pay day. From Fox's Lane, on the right, to the other side of the railway bridge, the trams were limited to a single track because of the narrowness of the road. On the left is Dunstall Street, with the tobacconist on the corner selling Gold Flake cigarettes for fourpence, as well as R. White's ginger beer and Fry's chocolate. Next door, with a dog hanging around on the off-chance that there might be some scraps, is S. N. Walley's butcher's shop. Beyond, on the left, is Ewins Street, with another tobacconist's shop occupying the corner site, and opposite is the dead-ended Moseley Street, with a public house on the nearest corner and the Stafford Road Bakery on the far side. Dominating the skyline are the chimneys of the railway works next to Brunel's masterpiece, which would be demolished in 1937; the road re-opened on 9 May 1937, when the whole length of Stafford Road could finally be converted to double-deck trolleybus operation. *J. Hughes collection*

Above Looking towards Five Ways from the Great Western Railway Institute railway bridge in Stafford Road on 30 December 1963, Sunbeam W4 trolleybus 436 (EJW 436) travels towards Fordhouses working on the 3 service. On the right, behind the leafless trees and between the terraces of railway workers' houses, is West Street, its name written on the gable end of a house whose style suggests that the road and the surrounding buildings date from before about 1865. The railway bridge is the steel structure that replaced the old brick-built Brunel skew bridge. The area in the bottom right-hand corner, where the road surface is cobbled, was known as Queen Square and led to Dunstall Hill Road. On the left is the retaining wall for the embankment of the GWR's Victoria Basin branch line, which took rail traffic to the Birmingham Canal Navigation's basin and the GWR's Goods Station, as well as that railway's line on to Shrewsbury. The only clearly readable advertisement on the wall is for Captain Morgan Rum. Today, only this blue-brick wall survives from this point to Five Ways, everything else having been demolished. Following the trolleybus is a Morris FG van with the unusual 'threepenny-bit' cab, a BMC Minivan and a Guy 'Arab' IV with a rear-entrance Metro-Cammell body, which is working to Bushbury Hill. *J. C. Brown*

Opposite below The tram tracks and the Lorain conduits were laid along Stafford Road during the warm summer of 1904. Just beyond the skew bridge at Queen Square, Stafford Road ran between the high-sided brick walls of the Great Western Railway's famous Stafford Road Works, which lay on both sides of the main road. This had been established in 1849 by the Shrewsbury & Birmingham Railway, and in the days of the Broad Gauge was taken over by the GWR, which continued to build locomotives there until 1908. The works finally closed in June 1964 with the loss of 500 jobs. The connecting enclosed works footbridge is visible on the left of the photograph. There are 39 men and boys posing for this photograph, which shows just how labour-intensive a job like track-laying was nearly a century ago. Everything was done with picks, shovels and crowbars to add to the brute force and sweat needed for such a task. This part of Stafford Road was an area of extreme contrasts: behind the GWR's works to the north-east was the site of the Wolverhampton Gas Company, while to the west was Dunstall Hill with its allotments, and a house called The Vinery, which had sunny west-facing glasshouses and just might have produced on its sloping land the beverage implied by its name! One wonders if the workmen would have appreciated the local drink to quench their thirst? Beyond Dunstall Hill was more open

land in the form of the Dunstall Park Racecourse with its associated local railway station. *Bennett Clark*

Below Stafford Road had to cross a number of canals and railways on its way to Bushbury and Oxley. At Gorsebrook Road, beyond the GWR's Stafford Road Works, it had to cross the Birmingham Canal Navigation, which was heading to nearby Aldersley Junction with the Staffordshire & Worcestershire Canal up a flight of 21 locks. It is difficult to imagine that until the Second World War the canal to Aldersley, about a mile away, was in the countryside. Modern urban expansion has largely filled the Smestow Brook valley through which the canals pass, although the flood plain is retained as a nature reserve, a rifle range and playing fields, as well as containing the Aldersley Stadium. Just beyond the canal bridge is Jones Road, named after Thomas Jones, a local brickmaker and entrepreneur, who was 'doing his bit' for urban expansion, just as was to happen 80 years later in Aldersley. On the right, behind the man hurriedly pushing his handcart, is the headquarters of the Wolverhampton Gas Company, which was unusual in that it was not municipally owned, as most were in the Victorian age. Just beyond the wall is the Bridge Inn with its later single-storey extension next to the canal bridge. On the left, just before Gorsebrook Road, are the 'concrete cottages' of 1876, which were so well-built that when they were declared unfit in 1966 they were extremely difficult to demolish. The group of people just beyond Gorsebrook Road are standing outside the corner shops squeezed against the western canal bridge parapet. The picture was taken between the conversion of the trams to the overhead current collection method in 1921 and the abandonment of the Bushbury trams in 1925. *J. Hughes collection*

Above Having just pulled away from the row of shops in Stafford Road near the junction with Showell Road, the driver of 439 (EJW 439) will have to coast across the power point before the end of the row of shops, or risk blowing the circuit-breakers in the cab. The trolleybus is yet another of the ubiquitous Roe-rebodied Sunbeam W4s that served the system so well in its last years of operation, and is travelling into the town on the 3 service on 23 November 1961. It will shortly pass the huge Electric Construction Company's factory, whose westerly extremities adjoined Stafford Road in the form of two workshops opposite the Co-op, just off the photograph to the right. The double-fronted Co-operative store stands on the corner of Showell Road into which a cyclist and a Morris Minor Traveller, first registered in March 1955, are turning. Next door is a dry cleaner and a shoe repairer, while behind the trolleybus is another small row of shops. A brief industrial 'star' burned brightly in Showell Road, as it was here, from 1929 until the receivers were called in during March 1932, that the Star Motor Company had its car manufacturing works. The mock-half-timbered building in the background, behind the one-year-old Standard Vanguard Vignale that is following the trolleybus, is The Croft public house, located on the corner of Bushbury Lane at the former tram terminus. *J. C. Brown*

Opposite above This much earlier photograph shows the same stretch of Stafford Road, looking towards the original terminus at Bushbury Lane, Oxley Bank. Beyond the shops on the left, by the lone cyclist and lady pedestrian and behind the trees, is the entrance to Oxley House, a rather large Regency house originally built for John Henry Sparrow, a local ironmaker. After a somewhat chequered history, it

survives today, having been converted into luxury flats in 1983. Almost opposite the cyclist is the junction with Showell Road, with the Wolverhampton Co-operative Society shop in its original two-window-bay form. The open-topped double-decker tram is standing at the Bushbury Lane terminus, which was reached on 13 August 1904, and at the time was about at the limit of Wolverhampton's northern urban growth along Stafford Road. This rural image was, however, something of an illusion, as the huge ECC factory had been established off Showell Road in 1890, not closing until 1985; one of the workshop buildings can be seen between the trees and the Co-op shop on the right. *J. Hughes collection*

Right The rural nature of Stafford Road in the Edwardian era is easy to forget nowadays! The trams were introduced on this route on a Saturday in the glorious summer of August 1904, as an extension to the north of the town from the Molineux football ground in Waterloo Road. At that time the Bushbury Lane tram terminus was almost in the countryside, as the row of neat garden-walled Victorian terraces beyond the Birmingham Canal were already about ten years old. Tram 14, an open-top double-decker with reverse staircases, built by G. F. Milnes and entering service in July 1902, stands at the end of the row of rather severe-looking houses, with the gas street lamp positioned on the corner of Bushbury Lane. The tram is showing the destination 'RAIL STATION'. Hidden by the trees is the large house that became The Croft public house, seen opposite, and through the tunnel of trees beyond the workmen and their cart are the 'stepped' terraces dating from 1900 on Oxley Bank, Stafford Road. *D. R. Harvey collection*

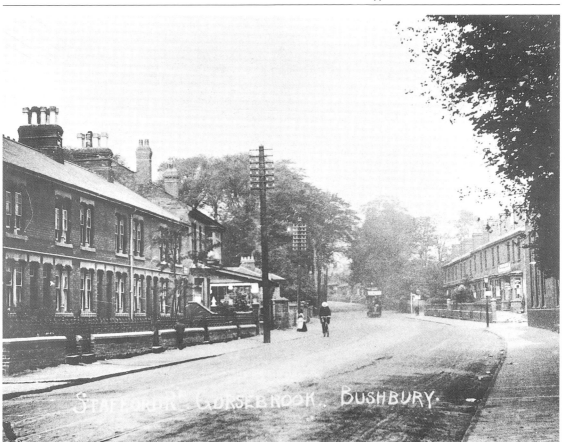

Right Having arrived at the Bushbury terminus, the crew of car 35, including Driver Jack Rogers, pose in front of their charge. The conductor has a money satchel strapped across one side of his chest and a Bell Punch ticket machine on the other, while he appears to be holding a wooden ticket rack. The photograph was taken between 1921 and 1925, when the trams working on the route, including car 35, were working on the overhead system. The tramcar was built in mid-1905 by the United Electric Car Company as a 51-seater open-top double-decker mounted on Brill 21E trucks, but in the years prior to the First World War was fitted with platform vestibules. The metal cowling behind the crew is to cater for the winding on or off of the horizontal handbrake wheel. *J. C. Brown collection*

Above When Bushbury Lane was developed, the land at the lower end nearest to Stafford Road was devoted to the new Goodyear factory. Further up, beyond the railway bridge over the former LMS railway line, it was developed as an adjunct to the Low Hill and Showell municipal housing areas in the late 1920s and 1930s. Typical of the type of house that was built were these blocks of four two-bedroomed houses. The bus working into the town on the 33 service, passing Whetstone Grove on the left and Wingfoot Avenue in the foreground, is 397 (FJW 397), a Guy 'Arab' III with a Brush 54-seater double-decker body. It entered service in early 1949 and is seen here when fairly new with a varnished dark grey roof. *D. Vernon*

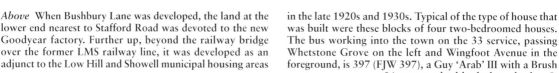

Left On 4 April 2002, a by now somewhat elderly Travel West Midlands MCW 'Metrobus' Mk II speeds away from the stop at the Broadway on Northwood Park Road. The bus is 2808 (B808 AOP), which entered service in November 1984 and, despite its 18 years, looks in remarkably fine fettle. The passengers on the upper deck can look to their left over the wide open spaces of Northwood Park and the Northicote Secondary School, with Cromwell Road and the old 41 service terminus. The present-day 533 service continues along Bushbury Lane as far as the well-hidden, partly medieval but mostly Victorian, Bushbury Church, before turning into Collingwood Road then, after another area of late-1940s municipal housing and a small shopping area, arriving at Northwood Park. *D. R. Harvey*

Right Quietly waiting at the terminus in Cromwell Road is a Brush-bodied Guy 'Arab' III, working on the 41 service, which, like the 33 route, went to Northwood Park but via the Woodbine Inn, rather than the clockwise 33, which went to the terminus by way of Bushbury Church. While the 33 service had been extended from Bushbury Church on 4 October 1948, the anti-clockwise 41 service left Bushbury Lane and turned into Fordhouse Road. The bus, for some long-forgotten reason showing the wrong destination display, is 387 (FJW 387), one of only six Guy 'Arab' IIIs to enter service in 1948. Fitted with a Gardner 6LW 8.4-litre engine and a composite-framed Brush H29/25R body, in this mid-1950s view the bus still retains its trafficators. 387 was to have a life of 19 years, surviving until 1967. *D. R. Harvey collection*

Below This is a most contentious photograph as it apparently shows the trolleybus turning circle in place at the Bushbury Lane and Stafford Road junction, but with the extension beyond the old tram terminus tied off because the wiring was not completed for use! The trams stopped running to Bushbury on 19 August 1924 and, after a short period of operation using hired motorbuses, the replacement trolleybus service was introduced on 9 March 1925. This photograph, taken just in front of The Croft public house, suggests that although the wiring for the extended service to Fordhouses was in place, it was not in fact brought into operation. The Bushbury Lane turning circle was made operational on 23 April 1925, but this evidence suggests that it was the original temporary trolleybus terminus. If that is true, then it was this that was in fact opened on 9 March, not the extension through Oxley to Fordhouse. As if to emphasise this anomaly, it was the extension that was given the modified route number 3A, while the Bushbury service retained the original tram route number of plain 3. The problem with this theory is that Arthur Baker's butcher's van, standing at the side gate of the 1920s-built shop, was registered in 1926! *J. Hughes collection*

Above The tree-lined Oxley Bank in Stafford Road actually had on its eastern side terraced houses, dating from 1900 and named after early skirmishes in the Boer War, seen here on the left. Looking down the hill towards the Bushbury tram terminus, with the Regency-period Oxley House on the right and the half-timbered Croft public house on the left, open-topped double-decker tram 33, working on the Lorain system, stands at the Bushbury Lane terminus. Behind the tram, another of the UEC-built cars bought for the extra traffic that the opening of the Bushbury service would afford, is the row of shops and houses leading to the ECC factory beyond the corner of Showell Road. This Edwardian view would remain little altered until the mid-1920s, when both municipal and privately owned houses would be built, which would extend the housing beyond the huge Goodyear Tire (the original US spelling) & Rubber Company's factory of 1927, in the angle of Stafford Road and Bushbury Lane. *J. Hughes collection*

Opposite This similar view is also looking towards the old tram terminus at Bushbury Lane, marked by the just visible pub sign for The Croft public house. 'Steaming' up Oxley Bank on 24 January 1964 is Sunbeam W4 trolleybus 451 (EJW 451). The shadowy outline on the horizon is the huge bulk of the ECC factory, which despite its imposing presence over Stafford Road was not the immovable industrial object it seemed, closing in 1985 after many years of fighting off economic collapse. The trolleybus is working out of town on the 3 service and is passing the 1920s-built council housing and the Oxley Avenue cul-de-sac. The trolleybus entered service on 26 January 1948 with a Park Royal H28/26R body, but was taken out of service on 11 November 1960 for five months while the old body was scrapped, and the chassis thoroughly overhauled and sent to Charles Roe of

Crossgates, Leeds, to be rebodied with the elegant style shown here. In this form it lasted until 5 March 1967, the final day of trolleybus operation in Wolverhampton. Although these were the second batch of trolleybuses to be rebodied by Roe, they were indistinguishable from the first group of 16, except in one significant matter – at £3,227 per body, they were £259 more expensive. The tall building on the right is the Dunstall Odeon, which opened on 19 November 1934 as the Dunstall Cinema and survived until 5 November 1960. Its first projectionist was Harry Baylis, who returned to operate the last showing, comprising the films *Savage Innocents* and *Dead Lucky*. By the time Cliff Brown had taken this photograph, the old picture house was reduced to the almost inevitable bingo hall, opening as such on 16 February 1962. It finally closed on 23 September 1981, succumbing to J. J. Gallagher's ball and chain and the impending Stafford Road widening scheme of 19 November 1981.

It is hardly possible to imagine that so much from 1964, let alone the first decade of the 20th century, has survived at Oxley Bank on the dual-carriageway of Stafford Road. Looking towards Wolverhampton city centre on 4 April 2002, the half-timbered Croft public house, overlooking the re-aligned junction with Bushbury Lane, is now renamed the Island House. Beyond the large traffic island that dominates the bottom of Oxley Bank the row of terraces housing the old Co-op shop in Stafford Road has been obliterated, while the once important Showell Road junction has lost its direct vehicular access. The once mighty ECC factory has long been demolished and replaced by an industrial estate. However, on the left the rows of 1900-built houses, albeit behind their replacement garden walls, still provide a certain quality along Oxley Bank, while opposite the 1920s former council housing survives. *J. C. Brown/D. R. Harvey*

Above Travelling along Stafford Road towards town on the 3 route from Fordhouses is trolleybus 447 (EJW 447), one of the Roe-rebodied Sunbeam W4s of 1948 vintage, which has stopped at the impressive bus shelters outside the administrative block of the giant Goodyear Tyre & Rubber factory in the days well before the A449 was made into a dual carriageway. The office block belongs to the last stage of the factory's 1960 expansion schemes and stood on the opposite side of the site from the main factory entrance facing Ripon Road, which ran between Stafford Road and Bushbury Lane. The building of the factory began in 1927, and by the mid-1960s was employing 5,500 people, although today it survives by employing a skeleton staff of a few hundreds. On the left is a Bedford CC-registered Ford Thames 305E 5cwt van dating from December 1959. *J. C. Brown*

Below The final turn-back point on Stafford Road before the terminus was at Oxley beyond the Goodyear factory. This was where Oxley Moor Road crossed the main A449, becoming Church Road to the east and within a mile of the Fordhouses terminus at The Vine. In the days before this section of Stafford Road was made into a dual-carriageway, a motor cyclist, on his already eight-year-old bike, takes a somewhat chary look at the circling trolleybus as he begins to make his turn into Oxley Moor Road. Behind the two schoolgirls and the telephone box on the far corner are rows of detached bungalows dating from that period of the 1930s when 'ribbon development' along main roads was beginning to impinge on undeveloped land at the edge of urban areas. Such bungalows and 'semis', with their round bay windows, were the catalyst for the start of the development of the Green Belt policy, first implemented in the Town & Country Planning Act of 1947. The trolleybus, 440 (EJW 440), a Roe-rebodied Sunbeam W4, has its destination blind turned already to the somewhat generic 'WOLVERHAMPTON' on 28 March 1961. *J. C. Brown*

Above A Morris Oxford Series V with a Farina-styled body speeds along Stafford Road near the junction with Three Tuns Lane and Marsh Lane, with a trolleybus bound for Fordhouses in close pursuit. The trolleybus is 442 (EJW 442), one of the rebodied Sunbeam W4s, and it is Wednesday 26 January 1964, the last day of operation on the Fordhouses route. Stafford Road is being widened to become a dual-carriageway, as the most direct way of getting to Stafford. In later years this widening became a huge advantage as it enabled traffic to come off the M54 from Shrewsbury and North Wales and gain access to the then thriving industry of northern Wolverhampton and the rest of the Black Country. On the right are all the accoutrements of road building, with a mobile crane – perhaps an Iron Fairy with rear-wheel steering – a road-roller and a Ford Trader 6cu yd tipper. Above the roadworks are the old hangers on the line of the original northbound single carriageway, while the trolleybus is using the temporary wiring that enabled them to continue running, albeit for a short period, until the abandonment date – despite appearances, the trolleybuses never ran on the completed northbound carriageway to Fordhouses. On the left a mother pushes her child in its pushchair past the Three Tuns Parade of local shops, having just been overtaken by a town-bound Austin A30 and an early Mini. Pursuing the trolleybus is an advanced Citroen ID 19 and a late Ford Prefect 100E. *J. C. Brown*

Right Looking at the junction from the opposite direction, today it is dominated by one of the largest public

houses in Oxley, the Mitchells & Butlers-owned Three Tuns public house, which although being a much later property, having been constructed in the early 1930s, stood on the site of a Georgian toll-house and inn. While the council and private 1930s housing along Stafford Road has remained only cosmetically altered, the land on the Marsh Lane side of the junction around the public house was developed during the 1960s with a rather severely styled shopping centre. This has left the pub looking like a large stately ship, in comparison with the surrounding buildings. On 4 April 2002 Travel West Midlands 38-seater Optare XL 687 (S687 YOL) has just come around the traffic island on the way into Wolverhampton, although the destination blind has not been reset for the inbound journey. *D. R. Harvey*

Below The 1930s semi-detached houses lining Stafford Road began just before the distant roundabout at Marsh Lane with its small shopping centre clustered around the junction. The trolleybus has just passed the last of the 1920s terraced rows at Newbury Road, as its driver has turned on the flashing indicator so that it can move out into the normal line it would take on the nearside of Stafford Road's

northbound dual-carriageway, this section having opened during the 1930s. The trolleybus is Roe-rebodied Sunbeam W4 448 (EJW 448), which is displaying the usual destination of '3, FORDHOUSES'. On the central reservation, together with the newly planted trees, are centre traction poles with bracket arms for each carriageway's set of wires. Following the trolleybus is a Ford Zephyr Mark I, with its straight-six

2,262cc engine, which gave it a top speed of just over 100mph and a reputation in some circles as 'the poor man's Jag'. Parked on the inbound carriageway is one the Zephyr's contemporary rivals, the wrap-round-windscreen Vauxhall Cresta PA, which also boasted a hideously styled three-piece rear window. Strangely, the engine capacity of the Cresta was also 2,262cc! *J. C. Brown*

Below left Negotiating the final traffic island along Stafford Road in November 1961 is Sunbeam W4 trolleybus 412 (DJW 412). This was numerically the second of the six trolleybuses to be repainted in the dark green with a single straw-coloured band at waistrail level. It retained this livery from December 1959 until March 1962, whereupon it was returned to the standard fleet colour, although it made little economic sense to do this expensive job as 412 was withdrawn on 3 November 1963. The trolleybus has set down all its passengers and is executing a 180-degree turn in order to reach the starting bus stop whose shelter can just be seen on the far side of Stafford Road above the roof of the Austin A55 van. In the foreground is Wobaston Road, along which, at Patshull Avenue, almost in sight of this Stafford Road traffic island, the 28 bus route through the Wobaston Estate terminated. The municipal housing around the terminus was built in the 1930s and as well as having The Vine public house on one side of the traffic island, diagonally opposite the needs of the local community were met by a small row of shops. Outside the shop on the extreme right is an early Wall's Ice Cream vending machine, looking remarkably like one of the contemporary Fresh Milk machines that served cardboard packets of ice cold pasteurised milk or the sickly sweetened strawberry-flavoured variety. *J. C. Brown*

Top Waiting at the Patsull Avenue terminus of the 28 service on the post-war Wobaston housing estate on Monday 12 May 1952 is Guy 'Arab' III 545 (FJW 545) in more or less its original condition. This fine study of shows that even among this batch of fairly standardised Park Royal-bodied buses there were differences specified by Wolverhampton Corporation, the most interesting modification being the sliding cab door. As mentioned opposite, this terminus was within easy walking distance of the turning circle at the end of the 3 trolleybus route at The Vine, Fordhouses. The service began on 9 April 1951, although it was extended to Wolverhampton Airport at Pendeford as the Mondays to Fridays-only 78 service. Today this area is largely built over with industry and housing. *J. C. Brown*

Above Back at the Fordhouses trolleybus terminus the Stoke-on-Trent-registered Morris Ten-Four of September 1934 dates the view nicely, when the Fordhouses terminus was still a very rural area. Although the trolleybuses reached here in 1925, the original 18-inch overhead wire spacing is still in situ nearly ten years later. This countryside idyll would be rudely broken by the impending Second World War and would not survive for much longer. Within a few years H. M. Hobson would built its aircraft components factory, later to become Lucas Aerospace, while the Wolverhampton-based Turner Manufacturing Company would open its new vehicle transmission and aerospace factory. The Vine, a turn-of-the-20th-century public house with its pleasure gardens, stands on the corner of Bee Lane, while the cluster of 18th-century cottages on the left are on the corner of Wobaston Lane, with Stafford Road disappearing into the countryside to the north of the town's boundary. *J. Hughes collection*

A mother and daughter sit on the bench alongside the simple bus shelter on a bright summer's day at the end of the 1950s. Next to them Park Royal-bodied Sunbeam F4 458 (FJW 458), which had entered service on 4 September 1948, is waiting at the Fordhouses terminus in Stafford Road, with Bee Lane and the half-timbered Vine public house in the background, both partly hidden behind the vehicle. The council housing, with its easily identifiable multi-paned windows, dates from the late 1930s as part of the large municipal housing developments of the inter-war period.

The trolleybus driver has already changed the destination display for the return journey via the town centre to Bushbury Hill. This trolleybus was the only one of the 99 8-foot-wide trolleybus never to be fitted with flashing indicators, managing to retain its semaphore arms until withdrawal on New Year's Eve 1961. It was also the only one of the Park Royal-bodied Guy BTs and Sunbeam F4s to keep its trolleybase shields, which although serving little practical purpose, did tidy up the external appearance of the roof by hiding the trolleybases and grease-covered tension springs from the gaze of the public.

The terminus has hardly changed since the demise of the trolleybuses. On 4 April 2002 Travel West Midlands Optare XL 686 (S686 YOL) is working on the 503W route from the Springfield Lane area, and has just negotiated the traffic island at the Vine to arrive at a somewhat more substantial, but mightily abused, modern bus shelter. The 1930s council houses have been upgraded by the fitting of double-glazing, but are substantially unchanged since the late 1950s. While the 38-seater Optare single-deckers are obviously smaller than the old 54-seater double-decker trolleybuses, the decline in passenger numbers has been such that they are more than adequate for the modern-day service, especially in view of the number of operators that run along Stafford Road. *A. Moyes/D. R. Harvey*

Buses beyond Fordhouses

Above Coming along Stafford Street in the large South Staffordshire village of Brewood, and about to enter the Market Place, also known as The Square, early in 1970 is 147 (DDA 147C). It has come into the village from Wheaton Aston, having crossed the busy A5 Watling Street at Stretton. The bus was the first vehicle from the first batch of Strachan-bodied Guy 'Arab' Vs; it entered service in February 1965 and survived until 1976. It was also one of eight of the first batch to be overhauled, but such was the state of their bodies that the cost of overhauling the remaining 33 was considered to be too great. On the right of this narrow street is the Lion Hotel, built on the corner of the Market Place, which was formerly the magistrates court and dates from about 1800. At the time that this photograph was taken, Brewood had just been designated an Outstanding Conservation Area, with its Georgian and medieval architecture. Today it has won several awards for being the best-kept village in South Staffordshire. *P. Roberts*

Above right The service to Brewood Square began on 16 August 1922, with a further extension to Stretton, Lapley and Wheaton Aston. By 1930 the cost of the journey to Brewood was ninepence. Standing just off the Market Place in Brewood on 26 January 1973 is AEC 'Reliance' 706 (706 CDA), with a Park Royal body of a dual-doored 40-seater layout, which has come into the village on the 22 route. It is about to depart for Wheaton Aston, where it will terminate. By this time the bus has been repainted in WMPTE livery. To the left, just off the picture, is the old pump and horse-trough, while just visible above the roof of the bus is the medieval Swan public house. *R. Smith*

The shortworking of the 22 service to Wheaton Aston was the 52, and waiting at the rustic wooden bus shelter in Sandy Lane, Brewood, is Park Royal-bodied Guy 'Arab' V 142 (142 DDA), which has just arrived from Wolverhampton. It is early 1970 and the bus is still in the Wolverhampton Corporation livery despite having been taken over by West Midlands PTE. It is still quite cold, as the bottom of the radiator grill has been stuffed with newspapers in order to get the water in the tubes a little bit warmer. Behind the bus is the sign of the Lion Hotel on the corner of Stafford Street, while in the background are the splendidly eccentric windows of the Georgian Speedwell Castle, built in about 1740, while to the left is The Square, where all the main shops of Brewood are situated.

The Great Wyrley-based Warstones Motors operates under the fleet name Green Bus Services, and serves a large area based on Cannock, Lichfield and Wolverhampton, also running to many of the South Staffordshire villages that were formerly in the territory of the erstwhile Wolverhampton Corporation. The 'bark' of the Leyland 'Leopard' may have been silenced in the fleets of Arriva and First Bus, but in the Green Bus fleet the roar is as loud as ever. On 4 April 2002, having turned into the Square from Stafford Street, 18 (EHG 44S), an East Lancs-bodied Leyland formerly in the Burnley fleet, stands in Sandy Lane at the bus shelter were the WCT Guy was seen 32 years before. It is working into through the village on its way to Coven and Wolverhampton. *P. Roberts/D. R. Harvey*

Waiting for passengers in the centre of the Staffordshire village of Wheaton Aston is yet again Park Royal B40D-bodied AEC 'Reliance' 706 (706 CDA). This vehicle was one of three single-deckers emanating from the London area manufacturer in September and October 1963, bought for use on the Cheslyn Hay and Churchbridge services, where low bridges remained a problem. 706, by now working as a general country bus for its new owners, West Midlands PTE, is standing alongside the churchyard wall of St Mary's, whose east window rises up above the single-decker. The 22 service was only to have a short life with WMPTE as it was one of the routes inherited from Wolverhampton Corporation that were taken over by Midland Red on 3 December 1973, when that company lost its Birmingham and Black Country 'heartland' services to the PTE, leaving villages such as

Wheaton Aston with a much less reliable service. St Mary's Church was consecrated in 1857, having been built by public subscription to replace a medieval chapel that was in grave danger of falling down. The church was designed by two architects, Messrs Bidlake and Lovatt, in a Gothic style that unfortunately lacked a decent spire or tower to complete the 'look' of the church, as seen in the present-day photograph.

The area around the church was landscaped and redesigned in the late 1990s so that where the buses used to terminate in School Road is little more than a pedestrian walkway. Although the churchyard wall remains, the road doesn't, and the Choice bus, which today serves Wheaton Aston, only travels on the road at the edge of the village, where the rooftops of the houses on the skyline can be seen. *R. Smith/D. R. Harvey*

Cannock Road country bus routes

Most of the Cannock Road services began in either the imposing surroundings of Wulfuna Street or Stafford Street, in and around the Technical College area. The exception were those that were classified as the 'country bus services', many of which originally started in Market Street or Railway Drive near the High Level Station, then, after 9 May 1960, in the new bus station.

The services along Cannock Road left by way of Stafford Street, then turned right into Cannock Road, where the only gap in the residential lining was provided by the small but easily flooded valley of the Smestow Brook. Unlike the urban development along the nearby Stafford Road, the Cannock Road 'corridor' was generally developed in successive rings of housing built in the 1930s and 1950s, with the newest housing being on

the town boundary, though it was not necessarily privately owned.

Beyond the boundary and the furthest extent of the municipal trolleybus services, the Cannock Road motorbus routes included the 21 to Cannock itself via Shareshill, which began on 1 January 1921 using solid-tyred Tilling-Stevens single-deckers, while there was also a service to Featherstone and the 40 route to Brinsford. The routes to Cheslyn Hay (which was reached on 6 January 1926 as part of a scheme to combat the operation of Holmes's buses, a local independent operator), Churchbridge, Bridgtown and Essington all branched off Cannock Road and headed north-eastward along Blackhalve Lane and into the Staffordshire countryside. All these so-called 'country' routes were transferred to West Midlands PTE on 1 October 1969 and were lost to Midland Red on 3 December 1973.

Below left The Cannock bus service was started on 1 January 1921 as a joint financial operation between the non-operating Cannock UDC and Wolverhampton Corporation. The latter opened the route with 30-seater Tilling-Stevens TS3As, but in the postwar years double-deckers were the norm. The 21 bus route to Cannock started in the 'country' bus station, opposite Chubb Street. Standing in the bus station is 134 (134 DDA), one of the Corporation's unique batch of Guy 'Arab' Vs that were bodied by Park Royal, and which could easily be identified by their large windscreens and their rounded upper saloon rear domes; 134 entered service in January 1964. With a chock under the offside front tyre, the bus is waiting to load up

with passengers before the long run to Cannock. Looking over the bus station, on the corner of Victoria Square, is the wonderfully exaggerated style of the Victorian Prince Albert Hotel. *A. J. Douglas*

Top This more general view of the Railway Drive bus station not only shows the Prince Albert Hotel, but also Chubb & Sons' five-storey Lock & Safe Company building. This was built in 1899, and after the company left the premises for a new, modern base in Wednesfield Road, the Chubb Building was refurbished in 1991 and opened as the Lighthouse Media Centre. The 'country' bus station was opened in May 1960, replacing the old bus stands in Railway Drive and Railway Street. Leaving the somewhat heavy-looking concrete bus shelters is 710 (NJW 710E), an AEC 'Swift' MP2R with a Strachan B54D body. It entered service in June 1967, but its life was short, being withdrawn in 1974 due to its poorly designed body. It is working on the one-man-operated 57 service to Essington, but fortunately – for the driver – it is empty. *A. J. Douglas*

Above Parked at the back of the Railway Drive bus station is 529 (FJW 529), a Daimler CVG6 with a composite-framed Brush H29/25R body that somehow looks older than its service entry date of March 1950. Some of these Daimlers were taken out of service as long ago as 1961, yet 16 of them, including this one, lasted into West Midlands PTE days. The bus is standing against the fenced wall overlooking the sidings to the north-west of Wolverhampton High Level Station. It is a cold, misty morning in mid-November 1966, and on the former LMS railway line, by now equipped with the catenary for the overhead 25,000-volt electric power cables, is a row of railway parcel carriages curving away towards the distant gasometer. 529 is filling up with passengers for the 55 service, which went to Cheslyn Hay by way of Essington and was another of the Corporation's country bus routes. This route was formerly numbered 19A and first served Cheslyn Hay via Essington on 6 January 1926, in order to combat competition by a Mr Holmes, a local bus operator. Although this was five years after the agreement with Cannock UDC, the service was pooled with those to Churchbridge and Bridgtown, just south of the A5 trunk road and about 2 miles south of Cannock itself. These three services left Cannock Road at the Primrose Lane island near the single-storey shops and headed off to the north-east by way of Blackhalve Lane, crossing Long Knowle Lane, which linked the Pear Tree trolleybus terminus with the old Amos Lane terminus, nearer to the former. *G. Smith*

Below Perhaps one of the strangest purchases by Wolverhampton Corporation was also one of its last. Having favoured the somewhat frail bodies produced by Strachan on double-decker Guy 'Arab' V chassis, then the dual-doored single-decker bodies on rear-engined Daimler 'Roadliners' and AEC 'Swift' chassis, the purchase of a solitary lightweight Ford R226 chassis was to say the least surprising. 720 (KUK 720D) was a 36-foot-long single-decker with a dual-door Strachan 'Pacesaver' body, which could accommodate 54 passengers plus some standees. The bus had a new livery layout with green window surrounds and a deep yellow band beneath the saloon windows, which produced a very pleasing vehicle. The set-back front axle and a door opposite the driver at first sight looked most useful, but boarding passengers had to climb three steps to gain access to the saloon, which manoeuvre was further impeded by the cowl for the forward-mounted engine. Unfortunately,

720 did not have semi-automatic transmission and, although having a fair turn of speed, was not liked by the drivers, who had to struggle with a gearchange that was rather like 'stirring porridge with a stick'. It was valuable later in life when it was increasingly used as a driver trainer, allowing new drivers to pass their driving test with an 'all-types' licence. The Ford survived until February 1977 in company with similar, though shorter, Ford R192s, which ran express services in WMPTE's South Division in Birmingham. It is seen parked in the bus station when new, awaiting its next turn on the 56 service to Cheslyn Hay. *R. J. Brooks*

Bottom Turning into the bus station from Railway Street is an inbound bus working on the 56 route from Churchbridge. Single-deckers were employed on these services because of the low railway bridges in the Cannock area. Having disposed of its still fairly new pre-war Daimler COG5 fleet with indecent haste, eight of which were sold during August 1944 as surplus to requirements, while the six COG5/40s of 1938 and 1939 lasted only until 1950, the Corporation bought five Park Royal-bodied and five Guy-bodied Guy 'Arab' IIIs, all with Gardner 5LW 7-litre diesel engines. The Park Royal buses were designed specifically for the Corporation, but a second batch of five was ordered for the Wolverhampton-Albrighton-Cosford service. These were the Guy-bodied vehicles whose bodies, looking very similar to the contemporary Burlingham bus body, were available more or less 'off the peg'. 563 (FJW 563), one of the Guy 'Arab' IIIs with a Guy B34R body, dated from 1949 and, in common with all ten of the post-war Guy single-deckers, was unusually specified with a Wilson pre-selector gearbox. After they entered service the road beneath the bridge on the 89 service to Cosford was lowered, making half of the virtually new single-deckers redundant at a stroke. *J. G. Simpson*

Right Speeding out of the bus station along Railway Drive in about 1961 is Daimler CVG6 518 (FJW 518), a Brush-bodied 54-seater that is seemingly well-laden as it works on the 21 service to Cannock. It is approaching Victoria Square and will then turn right into Railway Street. Parked in Railway Drive against the railway parapet wall is the penultimate bus of the first batch of 100 BMMO D7s. This Midland Red is 4176 (THA 176), which entered service in 1954. The heavyweight chassis of the D7 was coupled with a fairly lightweight Metro-Cammell H32/26R body, which in many ways was a precursor to the infamous 'Orion' bodies supplied successfully by the Metro-Cammell-Weymann group to operators across the country, not withstanding <?> Wolverhampton Corporation itself!

4177 is working on the 882 service to Stourbridge via Kingswinford and Wordsley, which route left the town by way of Penn Road and its trolleybus service. *R. F. Mack*

Below Travelling along Princes Street in the summer of 1959 is 563 (FJW 563) again. The 56 service from Churchbridge via Cheslyn Hay was originally numbered 19A, as was, confusingly, the shortworking service from Cheslyn Hay, and from its inception in 1926 used Market Street, which 563 is approaching, as its Wolverhampton terminus. To the right is Queen Street, which architecturally is probably the 'best' street in the town – certainly it is one of the most homogeneous, with many of its buildings dating from the Regency period. In the background, among the late-Victorian buildings behind the bus and the following Morris Minor 1000, is Princes Alley, which survives today containing a few shops and a restaurant. Once the 'country bus station' in Railway Drive had been opened, the service entered it by way of Railway Street. After withdrawal, 563 soldiered on, underused, until 1963, when it and its twin, 561, were converted to snowploughs for winter use, and mobile canteens for, nominally, the rest of the year, although in truth both spent much of their time gathering dust in the corner of Bilston Street garage, leading an even greater twilight existence until passing to West Midlands PTE and lasting until June 1971. *L. Mason*

Above Parked in Market Street is one of the unusually styled Park Royal-bodied Guy 'Arab' IIIs, 568 (FJW 568), loading up with passengers outside the rear entrance to Marks & Spencer's department store. The imposing front entrance to the store, which today is still one of the city centre's main shops, was in Dudley Street and dated from the 1920s. The bus is waiting to begin its journey to Churchbridge on the 56 route, which will take it through Cheslyn Hay. The first two buses of the batch were fitted with roof racks, which gave the already antiquated-looking body an even more pre-war appearance. All of the five, which were numbered 566-570, were at various times fitted with larger, more luxurious seats for use on the Corporation's country services, although it appears in this case that 568 is only equipped with standard bus seats. Within a few months the service to Churchbridge would be moved away from Market Street and into the new bus station at Railway Drive. 568 was the subject of an unsuccessful 'standee' experiment when double seats were replaced by singles to give more room. *A. J. Douglas*

Left Out in the country, having just arrived in the bus stop lay-by, AEC-engined Guy 'Arab' V 116 (7116 UK) is waiting at the village of Shareshill, on the A460 Cannock Road, between the present-day M54 Junction 1 and M6 Junction 11 in what still is a haven of Staffordshire countryside between these two motorway interchanges. It is the autumn of 1970 and the bus, which is working on the 21 service to Cannock, has been repainted into full West Midlands colours, even to the extent of having a khaki-coloured roof, which originated with wartime air raid camouflaging in the Birmingham City Transport fleet. It always seemed surprising that the Corporation should use double-deckers on the services into Staffordshire, but at various peak periods the number of passengers warranted their high capacity. *P. Roberts*

Above The 56 service went through Essington on its way to Bridgtown on a route that dated back to a Saturday-only service, begun on 5 May 1923, from Queen Square to the Minerva Inn at the village's centre. Guy-bodied Guy 'Arab' III 563 (FJW 563) appears to be on one of the post-war housing estates in the former coal-mining village, just over the hill from Hilton Main Colliery. Since the closure of the Cannock area coal mines the village has grown enormously, having increasingly become a Staffordshire dormitory settlement for the Wolverhampton area. In truth, why 563 is parked with its driver's door open and the saloon night blinds pulled down is a mystery – or perhaps it is not even in Essington, because further research suggests that it might be in the Cottage Lane area of Fordhouses. *J. Hughes collection*

Below Once beyond the boundary the open countryside beckoned and with the exception of the odd farmhouse and the villages of Shareshill, Laney Green and Longford, this was good farming land in the days before the M6 cut through the area at Sharehill. The precise location for this photograph is a bit obscure, but it appears to be between Sharehill and Cannock on what was to become the A460. The bus is number 28 (DA 9028), which was a Tilling-Stevens TS6 with a Dodson B36R body that entered service in December 1924. The conductor is wearing over his shoulders a leather cash satchel and a Bell Punch ticket machine, while the driver of this solid-tyred single-decker has a posture of someone who has been hauling a rather unwilling charge for an awfully long time. Between the bus crew's heads and below the cab windscreen is a wonderful cornet-like horn, so typical of the 1920s. Everyone is watching the photographer, even the two infants inside the bus. *D. R. Harvey collection*

Below The original terminus of the 21 service from Wolverhampton was in High Green, Cannock, quite close to the Market Place. Cannock was a product of the 19th century, only coming to prominence when coal was first mined. As a result most of the old town centre only dates from the middle of that century, although much was cleared and redeveloped in the 1960s. Here in the middle of the old shopping area, outside Marston's shoe shop, stand two of the stalwarts of the post-war bus fleet, Daimler CVG6 515 (FJW 515), delivered in February 1950, and behind it, and 10 months older, Guy 'Arab' III 6LW 396 (FJW 396). Both of these Brush-bodied buses have worked in on the 21 service. The advertisement for a Treble Chance win of £250,000 on Vernon's Football Pools suggests a date of about 1961, when a quarter of a million pounds was a lot of money. *A. J. Douglas*

Bottom Somewhat carelessly parked in the 1960s Stafford Road bus station in Cannock, which replaced the High Green street-parking town terminus, is full-fronted MCCW-bodied Guy 'Arab' IV 64 (4064 JW). It is on the 21 service and is loading up with passengers while the crew take a welcome break over a cup of tea and a cigarette in the bus station cafe. These 30-foot-long buses were extremely reliable, with most achieving more than 15 years in service, and 64 was one of the majority of the 40 Metro-Cammell-bodied buses to be repainted in West Midlands blue and cream. One does wonder, however, about the sanity of ordering a front-engined double-decker with a full front. It fooled no one into believing that it was a trolleybus (where are the poles?), and the garage fitters were not endeared to clambering in and out of cab doors to undertake the simplest task. It was also a fashion that dated very quickly, as the design somehow looked unfinished as if the draughtsman at the body-builder had run out of inspiration on that fateful Friday afternoon after lunch! Behind the Wolverhampton Guy is another MCCW-bodied bus, this time one of Walsall Corporation's MDH-registered AEC 'Regent' Vs, possibly working on the service from Hednesford. On the left is a Midland Red D7, which has come in from Stafford on the 836 route, while on the extreme left can just be glimpsed the ex-Guy Motors demonstrator 888 DUK, which by this time, with its ghastly Strachan bodywork, had failed to impress anyone save for the local undertaking and had been sold to Harper Brothers of Heath Hayes in May 1966. *A. J. Douglas*

Index of locations

Looking ahead to Part 3... The passengers begin to get off the trolleybus that has just arrived at the Leacroft Avenue terminus of the Bushbury Hill service in 1931, only about five years after this municipal housing estate had been begun. In the 1920s Wolverhampton expanded enormously and the Low Hill development eventually comprised some 5,250 houses. The Bushbury Hill 9A trolleybus service opened on the same Monday that HMV and Columbia records merged to form EMI, and the last of the five five-bay Dodson-bodied Guy BTXs that were placed in service in the first two months of 1930 was 66 (UK 7966), seen here. These 60hp vehicles were the first in the fleet to have a low-level rear platform. It is just unfortunate that Dodson's attractive bus body 'box' of the period was spoiled by having the driver's cab and front end tacked on to the vehicle with all the style of a wooden shed! *D. R. Harvey collection*